Compassion Reporting

Nia Andrews

Writing for me doesn't always mean it will resonate with my generation. So with that being said, if this lands in the hands of the future generations, you were in our thoughts along the way.

Preface

Why?" A simple question that has become an important part of my growth. It has always been there, guiding my curiosity as I journey through life. To say that "why" has been my guide is an understatement; it's the heart of my journey. As a writer, I'm connected to this curiosity, this need to explore without needing definite answers.

My life's path, like writing, hasn't been straight. It's gone through uncertainties, faced questions with no clear answers, and embraced the beauty of ongoing exploration. From my earliest memories, I've been fascinated by the world around me. "Why" has been my friend, driving me to learn, pushing me forward. This curiosity led me to discover my love for writing – a way to capture the connections between human experiences.

But I never thought writing would give me all the answers. The beauty of "why" isn't in finding answers, but in the journey itself. Every question leads to another, and in this process, I realized the joy is in the journey, not the destination. I've learned to enjoy the cycle of discovery, understanding that I don't need all the answers or definite conclusions.

I've come to see that my role isn't to find universal truths, but to understand the different viewpoints that make up our world. Curiosity helps me connect with people on a deeper level, seeing beyond the surface. It lets me enter places that might not be meant for me. Through curiosity, I can explore new territories and make connections that cross boundaries.

Even when I face judgment or criticism, my commitment to understanding "why" helps me not take it personally. Instead of finding fault, I try to understand the reasons behind their actions. This mindset shifts my focus from me to them, turning me into an observer and a listener, eager to learn.

And listening – it's such an art! It's been a part of me since I was young. A quiet act that shows empathy, understanding, and a desire to learn from the stories around me. Whether it's the wisdom of older folks or stories from my peers, every story adds to my understanding.

Listening fuels my curiosity. It shows that people can see the same thing differently. This idea, learned in my early years, led me to journalism. Curiosity became my compass, guiding me to untold stories that needed to be shared.

Through these stories, I aim not to find final answers, but to capture the essence of human experiences – emotions, circumstances, and viewpoints. Each encounter is a chance to understand the "why" behind the stories I record. These narratives are my way of celebrating the complexity of life and the richness of our collective journey.

In the big picture of life, my commitment to "why" remains strong. It has guided me through experiences, thoughts, and the stories of people I've met. While some seek answers and closure, I love the ongoing journey. Being a writer isn't about having all the answers; it's about the questions that keep me moving forward. "Why" has taught me that life's beauty isn't in having all the answers, but in the never-ending wonder that pushes us ahead.

Introduction

I am a trained journalist by profession and a career publisher with a specialty in intellectual property. I have formulated a method for sharing data storytelling.

Of course, I didn't desire to write an entire book on data storytelling, as much as I desired to write a book on what landed me here and I realized in creating the IPAR Method that the root or foundation to designing this method was compassion, but before we get there, data storytelling, Data adds credibility, context, and emotional depth to stories. It's like evidence that makes the story more convincing. When you use data, you're not just saying things – you're showing them with facts, numbers, and context. Data makes the story relatable by turning numbers into personal stories. It also strengthens arguments by providing evidence. And those charts and graphs? They help everyone see the big picture. So whether you're talking about serious topics or fun ones, data boosts your storytelling and makes it more solid and persuasive.

During my time as an undergraduate student, I took a class focused on data analysis, primarily centered around the utilization of census results in news stories. This experience left me with the conviction that data could serve a much broader purpose.

After completing my undergraduate studies, I ventured forth to find my niche in journalism. Although I initially considered pursuing graduate studies in sociology, my path shifted after working for an association dedicated to public health concerns. This experience led me to delve into secondary education classes because I wanted to engage more with the youth. However, I still believed that more needed to be done to connect with and impact communities effectively.

Recognizing the potential of engaging with youth and future leaders, I embarked on a journey that ultimately led me to law school to study intellectual property. In this process, I also fulfilled a childhood aspiration by starting my own magazine. This move felt right, as the language spoken there was one I understood deeply: ownership.

Now, how does this tie into data storytelling? I'm glad you asked. The data itself forms the story that needs to be brought to life. For underserved communities, it's time to utilize this data to craft and the true narratives. Although this method can be universally applied, its design is particularly aimed at empowering those whose voices struggle to be heard. It equips them with the skills to use technology, trends, and a universal style that can be adapted across various platforms for effective storytelling.

What led me to this point? Much credit goes to my time at Lurie Children's Hospital, and later at Northwestern University's Feinberg School of Medicine, Buehler Center for Health Policy and Economics. There, I served as a communication coordinator for the Illinois Violent Death Reporting System and Statewide Unintentional Drug Overdose Reporting Systems. These systems collected death data from diverse sources. While my role involved sharing findings through tools like data briefs and fact sheets, as a storyteller, I found this insufficient. My frustration arose from the belief that I couldn't adequately convey the value of the data and its potential to effectively narrate the stories of those who passed away prematurely.

Empathy involves understanding and sharing others' feelings, while compassion encompasses sympathy and concern for their hardships. These qualities often intersect, but compassion is enriched by knowledge and understanding. It's about knowing, and that knowledge empowers us to offer support and assistance in the areas we've invested in uncovering, researching, and reporting.

My objective is to remind journalists, writers, and information providers of the kind of compassion that should guide our work. First and foremost, we must recognize the essential role we play in a democracy. Despite the allure of sensational news, our duty is to gather, investigate, analyze, and report news and information to the public. Journalists hold a pivotal role in informing society, promoting transparency, and holding those in power accountable.

In a media landscape tainted by sensationalism and misinformation, compassionate journalism serves as a vital counterbalance. By prioritizing accuracy, fairness, and empathy, journalists provide a dependable and ethical alternative. This ultimately contributes to a discerning and well-informed public. Through compassionate storytelling, journalists possess the capacity to foster understanding and unity among diverse groups. By offering unbiased and empathetic coverage, they can dismantle stereotypes, confront biases, and cultivate a more inclusive society.

As a member of a marginalized group, I've observed a troubling absence of empathy and honesty in stories, particularly when addressing crime and violence in Black and Brown communities.

Let's begin by addressing crime and violence. While I believe there may have been strategic decisions at play, I'll refrain from delving into conspiracy theories, reserving that discussion for later chapters. Instead, let's rewind to around August 26th, 2006. Some of you might recall Hurricane Katrina. This catastrophic storm struck the Gulf Coast, causing a breach in a levee on the Industrial Canal near the Orleans and St. Bernard Parish Line. This breach led to flooding in the 9th Ward of New Orleans, Louisiana.

I, being from the Midwest and unfamiliar with hurricanes, was deeply affected by the reports and videos showcasing people in danger due to the storm. Watching the aftermath of Hurricane Katrina and the subsequent reports of bringing "refugees" to Chicago stirred a sense of obligation within me. Despite being a single parent and an undergraduate student with limited funds, I rushed to purchase supplies for these brave individuals who had lost everything.

Upon arriving to donate the supplies, I found that volunteers were needed to set up the relief efforts. I readily agreed, not realizing that this decision would significantly alter the course of my career.

At that moment, I didn't disclose my status as a journalism student. I was simply a concerned citizen, and this experience would later prove pivotal in shaping my path. If left me feeling empty and confused, because what would I do, how would I do it and how do I tell people I am doing whatever it was? But it's when I landed on my why, to make every decision in my life with a greater purpose.

Chapter One: Compassion Helps Us All

You know, compassion is like the glue that holds us all together in this big ol' world. When we take a moment to understand where someone's coming from and show that we care, it's like magic – building trust, friendships, and a real sense of community.

Think about it: when we're empathetic and get where others are coming from, it's like we're giving them a virtual hug. It's not just about us and our stuff; it's about recognizing and supporting the struggles and wins of our others around us. And that's pretty darn cool.

But here's the great part – compassion isn't just about being all warm and fuzzy. It's the secret to building trust. When we show that we're not just looking out for ourselves, it's like we're building a trust bridge. And trust? Well, that's the VIP pass to building deeper connections and patching up those awkward divides.

You know what though? Compassion is a two-way street. When we spread kindness like confetti, it's not just the receiver who's getting the good vibes. We're boosting our own happiness levels, too! It's like we're tapping into our inner superhero – the one who's all about doing good and feeling awesome.

So, imagine a world where compassion is the superstar. It's a place where kindness rules the roost, where arguments get resolved with understanding, and where everyone's got each other's back. Sounds good, right?

But let's not forget, we're all human, and we've got our quirks. Some folks say we're wired to look out for number one. And while that might be true to some extent, it doesn't mean compassion's out of the picture. We can totally balance our own needs with looking out for our neighbors. It's like finding that sweet spot between treating ourselves and sharing the love.

There's also this concern that being too compassionate might lead to people becoming couch potatoes. Always putting others first can make us forget about our own growth and happiness. But, hey, it's about finding that chill zone where we can help out without losing sight of our own journey. It's all about that balance, my friend.

Sure, compassion might not solve everything – we're not living in a fairy tale. Sometimes, things get really complicated, and good intentions alone won't cut it. That's when we whip out the big guns like critical thinking, compromise, and negotiation skills. Combining these tools with our compassion superpower? That's the real winning combo.

So, yeah, compassion works. It's the key ingredient to cooking up a world that's warm, fuzzy, and full of awesome connections. Let's sprinkle that stuff everywhere and see the magic happen!

I reside in a rural area just outside of Chicago that is often considered a suburb. However, we take pride in our country atmosphere and our deep connection to the land. Livestock sightings are a common occurrence when driving through the area. The air here is noticeably fresher and crisper due to the abundance of trees. We are fortunate to witness a variety of animals, and our region is known for spotting white deer, which adds to the charm of our country environment.

Living in a rural community, it is no surprise that there is a predominance of Republican and conservative ideologies. This doesn't pose a problem for my family, as we are accustomed to being surrounded by individuals who have different perspectives and backgrounds. We often find ourselves in shared spaces with people who have contrasting beliefs, cultures, and interests. While our politics may not always align, we can still find common ground in shared experiences. For instance, during the fall season, fresh markets open, offering a wide array of vegetables, plants, and seasonal items like pumpkins. Corn, especially sweet corn, is a popular commonality.

One day, I visited a farm stand and parked my small Fiat behind a pickup truck that was adorned with various Trump paraphernalia. Despite being used to conflicting views, I couldn't help but notice the display, especially in these politically charged times. As I approached the stand, I began browsing the produce, particularly the corn. I noticed that the man next to me, covered in Trump gear, was also selecting corn. Making conversation, I casually remarked, "You're a fan of the corn as well. Sweet corn is in season." We engaged in a friendly three to four-minute discussion about corn, which unexpectedly created a social bond between us. This experience made me reflect on the role of the media in fostering connections among people. Rather than constantly highlighting our differences, media organizations should focus on narratives that bring us together and promote social cohesion. By doing so, we can thrive as communities.

In my everyday life, relying on scripture to navigate through challenges is normal for me. Initially, I hesitated to use the word "qualified" because in life, I often take calculated risks for which I may not feel fully qualified but prepared enough to attempt. The circumstances leading up to such decisions make me believe that I can succeed, even without the proper credentials or background. Compassion is a different concept altogether. It doesn't necessarily require physical touch or action; it is primarily about the truth within oneself and how it translates into treating others. Compassion can be defined as the feeling that arises when faced with another person's suffering and the motivation to alleviate that suffering.

When writing about people's suffering, it is essential to tell the whole story, including its roots. In Chapter Two, we will delve into this aspect and analyze the data, ensuring that those who have been marginalized, oppressed, shunned, silenced, and ostracized have a stake in the narrative that aims to relieve their suffering. If we bring farming into the conversation, we must address the numerous changes occurring in this industry. News stories often highlight the injustices faced by farmers and how they are overlooked or forced to start over. However, what concerns me the most is the lack of discussion about black farmers. Do people acknowledge their struggles? Are there conversations about Pembroke, Illinois, which happens to be the most impoverished city in the state and has a strong farming presence? Pembroke is one of the oldest black rural townships, founded by a runaway slave named Pap Tedder before the Emancipation Proclamation. It is crucial to have meaningful conversations about what is happening in Pembroke and the challenges faced by black farmers.

The museum, located in Pembroke Township, is a rural black community with a population of around two thousand. It is situated sixty-five miles south of Chicago and is one of the largest of its kind north of the Mason-Dixon line. However, it is also one of the poorest areas in the country. Many black farmers settled in this region during the Great Migration, as they found Chicago to be overcrowded and inhospitable. They were able to purchase land in Pembroke Township at low prices, although the poor soil made it difficult to establish profitable farms.

According to the most recent census report analysis of Pembroke Township in Kankakee County, the population is currently 1529. The median age is 51, with 20 percent of the population falling between the ages of 60 to 69. The second highest age group is 10 to 19, comprising 15 percent of the township population. The population is almost evenly split between males and females, with 51 percent identifying as male and 49 percent as female. 77 percent of the population identifies as Black, and 70 percent earn less than fifty thousand dollars per year. Additionally, 24.3 percent of the population falls below the poverty line.

The introduction of the Nicor Pembroke pipeline has been seen by some as a potential solution to the challenges faced by the community. The Illinois Commerce Commission has approved a certificate of public convenience and necessity, allowing Nicor Gas to expand its service territory to include Hopkins Park and Pembroke Township. This would involve constructing the necessary facilities to provide natural gas to the area. Supporters of this initiative include local leaders, such as Pembroke Township Supervisor, Hopkins Park Mayor, and State Representative and Senator. National organizations like Rainbow PUSH and businesses like Nicor Gas are also involved in supporting this effort.

However, there are concerns and protests from residents of Pembroke Township regarding the pipeline. These residents are advocating for renewable energy sources rather than relying on fossil fuels. Unfortunately, media coverage has portrayed the community as resistant to the assistance offered by the government and the gas company, perpetuating a narrative that overlooks their true story. On the other hand, when we observe farming areas in the Midwest, we readily recognize the need for funding and support for farmers. This is also true for the people of Pembroke, who depend on their land's resources and strive to preserve its historical significance.

This has been ongoing for years, garnered by the help and unbalanced media reporting. Communities built by people who had nothing and turned it into something, communities had been destroyed; the deterioration of many black communities has taken place over the years, with factors such as gang violence, drugs, and other issues contributing to their decline. This decline has been particularly noticeable among communities that were once centers of black excellence, such as Bronzeville in the Chicago area.

Bronzeville was a thriving cultural and political capital for African Americans from the 1910s to the 1940s. It rivaled Harlem and was known for its bustling activity, nightclubs, and music scene, including jazz, blues, and gospel. The name "Bronzeville" is said to have originated from African Americans' skin color, which was closer to bronze than black. The decline of Bronzeville occurred after the end of racially restricted housing, leading to the departure of upper and middle-class families and the rise of poverty and overpopulation.

Today, efforts are being made to rebuild Bronzeville and preserve its historical landmarks. Black heritage tours are available, allowing visitors to explore the remaining architectural landmarks and learn about the community's rich history. Neighborhood groups and business interests are actively working towards revitalizing Bronzeville as a center of African American commerce and art. The current population of Bronzeville is approximately 24,919, with a median age of 34. Most residents are U.S. born, and there is a significant presence of white-collar workers in the area. Economic development projects, such as Northwestern Medicine's planned advanced outpatient care center, are expected to contribute to the community's growth.

We take pride in areas like Bronzville because they have withstood challenges by utilizing resources such as Black news organizations in Chicago that continued to share their stories, as well as resilient business owners who refused to give up and prevent their community from experiencing the violence and drug problems that plagued others. However, it is important to note that this example of unity and resilience is not the norm, but rather an exception. The media has played a role in highlighting and perpetuating the decline of these communities, rather than emphasizing the potential for improvement. While it is acknowledged that the deteriorating state of these communities is not solely the fault of the youth, but rather due to the lack of resources, the media's portrayal instills fear using young people. I believe that if we take the time to understand and empathize with the struggles faced by young people, it will allow us to approach the situation with compassion and understanding.

I have a story about a time when it was crucial for me to connect with young people in order to fully understand the work, I was doing with them as a mentor in the field of journalism. After leaving my job in 2010 to start my own publishing company and magazine, I decided to pursue further education in secondary education so that I could teach journalism to youth. As part of this journey, I took a few classes and had the opportunity to cover an event at a joint agreement school that included an alternative school within it.

During this event, the superintendent asked if I would be interested in becoming a paraprofessional, which is someone who supports the teacher in the classroom to ensure a balanced student ratio and provide assistance when needed. I applied for the program and obtained the necessary certification. This experience also served as an externship for my college education in secondary education.

I vividly remember my first day meeting the students after receiving training and having group discussions with the teachers. Many of the teachers were new to the profession.

For those unfamiliar with alternative schools, they are programs operated by local or regional boards of education that offer a non-traditional educational setting. These schools address the social, emotional, behavioral, and academic needs of students who have not been successful in regular schools, often due to behavioral issues or learning disabilities.

So, as I was sharing, on my very first day, I vividly remember being at home and contemplating what to wear. I was in my mid-20s and about to embark on an experience with high school students. It was important for me to dress appropriately, adhering to the dress code, while still seeming relatable to the kids. So, I opted for khaki pants, a blouse, and flat ballerina shoes - a typical outfit you would find at a store like Kohl's. At the time, my hair was cut short and growing out into a little afro. So, there I was, a 5'3, 150-pound individual, entering a classroom with students who were said to have behavioral issues.

As I walked into the building, the teachers were directed to the gymnasium where tables were set up with classroom numbers. Unfortunately, I ended up being assigned as the paraprofessional for the class that contained the infamous student everyone warned about. I was eager to see who this person was, someone with a big personality and a reputation for being aggressive. I felt a little intimidated.

Sitting at the table, I watched as the students began to enter the building. It was customary for me to stand up and acknowledge them, as I had been taught to do in my own personal experiences. It was a simple gesture to let them know that they were seen and valued. So, with a smile on my face, I stood up and waited for them. And then, there she was - the student everyone had been talking about. She yelled at me, asking if I was her teacher. I calmly replied that I was not her teacher but rather the teacher assistant. I introduced her to her assigned teacher, and from that point on, chaos ensued.

The social worker came to assist, guiding the student through her turbulent emotions. Meanwhile, the teacher and I focused on getting to know the other students, explaining our roles and what the school year would entail. The rest of the students were fairly typical for a first day - curious and trying to make sense of the situation. We navigated through the day, establishing a level of respect as new professionals, and set the tone for the rest of the school year. Overall, it was a normal and expected experience when dealing with teenagers on their first day.

I wanted to enter the school environment in order to understand and mentor youth with a fair and balanced approach when covering stories about behavioral and societal issues involving younger generations. I knew that my experiences in the classroom and at the school would greatly impact my future work, so I made a conscious effort to be fully present and engage with each day. I understood that in order to create an accurate narrative, I needed to fully experience and build relationships with the teachers, students, and have a clear understanding of the environment.

So here I am days into the school year, about two weeks, and I just had my first encounter with a conflict within the school.

This incident allowed me to witness how the school handled chaos. Let's go back a bit - I previously mentioned an aggressive young lady who seemed to have issues with the school environment. As I continued building relationships with the students and helping them navigate through their high school experiences and classes, I realized that they adjusted to the environment quickly. Surprisingly, even the seniors in the Home Room I worked in adapted well, despite the work being below their grade level. They were determined to focus, complete their education, and graduate.

One day, when I arrived for work, the teacher informed me that I had to attend a training session. So, I went to the gymnasium where the training was taking place, signed in, and collected the necessary materials. It turned out to be a physical training conducted by the police department called ***Devereux*** restraint trainer. This training was specifically for dealing with special needs students, some of whom had autism. The aim was to teach teachers how to protect themselves when faced with situations like a child engaging in head-banging or attempting to harm others with a pencil. It was understandable, but then we moved on to restraint training, which involved taking down an enraged student using various techniques. The purpose of this training was to ensure the safety of teachers, students, and other staff members. I was paired with a large, masculine police officer who showed me how to successfully restrain a student. While I followed the proper techniques, I couldn't help but feel uneasy about having to do this to students. Nevertheless, I realized that it was better for us as teachers to handle such situations rather than involving the police, as teachers have a better understanding of their students and youth in general. So, I concluded that the training was necessary and being given to the right people, considering the teachers were the ones in the classrooms. I completed the restraint training course and received my certificate.

However, that was not the only encounter that made me realize the struggles that our youth face. There are many issues that we tend to overlook, and we often fail to understand their experiences or how they internalize them. Another encounter involved a student in my classroom where the use of restraint became necessary. A group of male paraprofessionals restrained the young man, with two holding him down and two others standing nearby. This incident took place in the hallway while most of the class remained in the classroom. I caught a glimpse of what was happening outside, and it deeply affected another student, causing her to become upset and express her disapproval of the situation. She believed it was wrong, unfair, and likened the treatment of students to that of animals. She passionately defended the actions of the restrained student. Despite my efforts to calm her down and my established rapport with her, I was unable to bring her back to a calm state. Eventually, a social worker who had a stronger relationship with her intervened, took her to his office, and had a conversation with her. She returned to class later in the day, as students always go back to the homeroom before dismissal. I sat down with her, and we talked about what she had witnessed. She expressed a need to decompress from the experience, although I was hesitant as I did not want her emotions to escalate again. However, I realized the importance of allowing her to decompress and share her thoughts and feelings. During our conversation, she revealed that she had witnessed her sibling being restrained by the police and shot in the street when she was a young girl. This traumatic event had a lasting impact on her, and she had never received proper counseling or therapy to address it. Seeing the young boy on the floor in the hallway surrounded by the four men triggered her protective instincts and desire to defend him. Understanding her past experiences and the unresolved emotions they caused helped me comprehend her behavior and approach to certain situations. It made me question whether other young people have had the opportunity to decompress and confide in someone they trust. Without this support, they may find themselves in challenging circumstances that are often sensationalized by the media. These portrayals unfairly label them as monsters or nuisances, without considering the complete story or the underlying reasons for their behavior. It is important to recognize that such moments only showcase the worst of a person and do not define who they truly are.

In a later chapter, I will share my experience working in data surveillance and how it relates to the use or lack of data by the media. One significant finding I made while reporting on violent death data is the disproportionate focus on violence within inner cities, while rural crimes are rarely discussed. This discrepancy is partly due to the smaller population and lack of local news organizations in rural areas, which is a major issue within our communities. However, if we truly want to evaluate crime and create safer living spaces, it is crucial to examine the different types of crimes, the targeted victims, and the motives across all areas. This comprehensive approach is the only way public health initiatives can effectively eliminate violent crimes.

In a later chapter, I will delve into the fascinating world of data surveillance and share my personal experiences working in this field. Through my exploration, I will shed light on how data surveillance practices interweave with the media's utilization, or lack thereof, of data. One revelation that stands out from my time reporting on violent death data is the alarming disparity in attention given to violence within inner cities compared to the lack of discourse surrounding rural crimes.

While there are those who argue that covering violence in the news is crucial for safety reasons, it is worth questioning whether this approach has genuinely enhanced the security of any community. Studies indicate that news organizations often portray violent crimes in a manner that instills fear and causes individuals to greatly overestimate the prevalence of violence in their own neighborhoods. Moreover, these organizations tend to disproportionately highlight crimes occurring in moderately impoverished areas with limited resources, inadequate access to food, and a scarcity of businesses. Consequently, this biased reporting perpetuates stereotypes and fosters negative perceptions about the residents of these communities.

An illustrative example of this occurred during the George Floyd protests. While there were revelations of bad actors participating in these protests through investigative reporting, there was a group of teenage students in a local community who wanted to show solidarity with Black people by joining marches in different areas. They aimed to symbolize their unwavering support beyond the tragedy of George Floyd's murder. However, when the adults became aware of this, they started discussing in their chat groups that the groups marching in these communities were violent. This perception was shaped by mainstream news organizations reporting that many protestors were engaging in violence. Consequently, the adults felt it necessary to arm themselves and stand along the route they marched to intimidate the marchers in support of the Black Lives Matter movement.

It's not complex to understand that thinking about the plight of others and operating from compassion can be difficult, but if we genuinely aspire to comprehensively assess crime and cultivate safer living environments, it becomes imperative to examine the various types of crimes, the targeted victims, and the underlying motives across all geographic areas. This holistic approach is indispensable in our pursuit of effective public health initiatives aimed at eradicating violent crimes.

By broadening our scope beyond the boundaries of urban centers and acknowledging the prevalence of crime in rural areas, we can gain a more accurate understanding of the complex dynamics at play. This enhanced comprehension will enable us to develop targeted strategies, allocate resources appropriately, and implement preventive measures that address the root causes of violence in both urban and rural settings.

Chapter Two: Getting to the Root

"Getting to the bottom of things has its way of actually put you at the top."

The real deal behind many of the problems in America, and possibly globally, is a combo of greed and racism. They're like two peas in a pod, you know? Greed comes first, driving people to hoard wealth and power, caring zip about others. Then we've got racism, which is like the messed-up belief that one race is better than the others. These two troublemakers team up to make inequality and injustice a never-ending party.

Greed, that craving for more money and stuff, makes people and institutions shove everyone else aside to fill their pockets. It's like a rollercoaster of sucking up resources, leaving others high and dry. This drive for more ends up deepening economic divides, making society more unfair, and tearing us apart.

Now, racism, that's a nasty belief system that's been around forever. It's like thinking one group is aces and the rest are meh. This has been used historically to create a hierarchy where some groups get the upper hand while others get stepped on. And guess what? This messed-up system helps the greedy stay on top by keeping others down. It's like a partnership from hell.

These two bad actors create a vicious cycle. Greed pushes people to exploit and discriminate, and racism gives them a reason to justify it. And boom, we're stuck in a cycle of inequality that's hard to break free from.

To tackle all the mess, we gotta face up to greed and racism together. It's like dealing with a combo deal at the store – you can't just pick one. We gotta change the systems that make greed rewarding and dismantle the racist ideas that keep it going strong.

This isn't just about laws and policies – though those are important. It's about changing how we think and getting everyone on board. We gotta trash the divisions that have been built up and start valuing everyone, no matter their skin color.

To really fix things, we need to take on greed and racism like a tag team. It won't be easy, but it's the only way we can build a fair and equal future. So, let's drop the act, break the cycle, and make a world that's not ruled by greed and racism.

After graduating from college, I initially pursued a career in journalism. However, my path took a slight detour when I encountered the victims of Hurricane Katrina who had relocated to Chicago. This experience made me reevaluate my desire to be a journalist and the way I approached the field.

I had always envisioned myself as a broadcast journalist and enrolled in Columbia College Chicago right out of high school in 2001. I enjoyed studying and working in broadcast journalism, gaining a fresh perspective on various issues. Growing up in a marginalized community in Chicago and later moving to the suburbs gave me a diverse viewpoint on how things looked.

While taking writing classes at Columbia College Chicago, I found myself conflicted in storytelling. I felt that the narratives being presented often lacked a genuine depiction of the communities they were discussing. While I acknowledged the issues these communities faced and agreed with the available data, I believed that the lived experiences of the people from these communities were not adequately represented.

Reflecting on my own upbringing in Englewood, I realized that my day-to-day environment was centered around family- oriented individuals who worked hard, loved each other, and fostered a sense of community. There was a desire to provide for one's family, strive for improvement, and prepare future generations. Our community was built on connections and knowing our neighbors. It was about navigating the American experience while embracing our own culture, influenced by hip- hop and creating our unique community.

However, I also witnessed the dismantling of this community by the rise of gangs, drug use, and drug sales among the younger generation. This contrasted with the values and actions of the older generation, particularly my grandfather's generation. They were connected to trades, married, raised children, and served as pillars of the community. They embodied the ideals of manhood and were a source of guidance and advice.

The younger generation seemed to rebel against these moral standards, engaging in activities for quick money like drug selling. They formed blocks within the community, with specific gangs exerting control. I observed this shift occurring in the late 80s and early 90s, because of the older girls on the block dating individuals from other areas. Consequently, some parents felt compelled to move their children away from these experiences to provide them with a more equitable upbringing separate from that lifestyle.

Living in that community, I learned the importance of community, love, and the southern hospitality that stemmed from the great migration movement. These narratives often get left out, overshadowed by other stories in the media. As black individuals, we still have our own culture and values that are significant to us. For instance, we hold our mothers in high regard, upholding them like queens, which may differ from other cultures' perspectives. These details about our identity, what we stand for, and what we're willing to fight for often get buried in media narratives.

Additionally, the role of black men as patriarchs and their contributions in shaping our communities is an aspect that is often overlooked. Without the strength and decisions of black men, many disinvested communities would not have existed. These stories deserve to be brought to light and recognized.

However, I want to circle back to my point about journalism and how I veered away from my original plan of pursuing broadcast journalism. The reason for this deviation was because I realized that our stories were not being accurately, truthfully, and impartially told. This realization occurred during my first two years of studying journalism, prompting me to take some time off.

During my break, I had the opportunity to volunteer with the victims of Hurricane Katrina who had been relocated to Illinois, from Louisiana. While working alongside other volunteers, including local news reporters, we were busy preparing the facility for the victims of the hurricane. In the process, we bonded and shared our own stories of triumph and the reasons that brought us to volunteer.

At this point, I hadn't mentioned that I was studying journalism, and I wasn't viewing the situation as an opportunity to advance my career. It was simply about being present, connecting with people, and providing support. I refrained from sharing my educational background and my disappointment in how journalism was being practiced. The classes I had taken didn't equip me with the necessary tools to tell stories accurately, which conflicted with my beliefs.

One pivotal moment occurred when a bus arrived carrying tired individuals who were disoriented and had very few belongings. To my dismay, reporters rushed towards them, shoving microphones in their faces and asking about their stories and journey. They referred to these individuals as migrants. Witnessing this behavior disgusted me and made me realize that I didn't want to be part of a reporting system that lacked empathy and sensationalized stories.

Upon returning to Columbia, I had already completed two and a half years of my degree, with a year and a half remaining. However, due to financial constraints, I had to take a break to gather funds for my education. Upon resuming my studies, I decided to change my concentration to magazine article writing. I believed this avenue would allow me to delve deeper into stories, engage in authentic conversations, analyze data, provide commentary, and shed light on various communities and issues.

In journalism, it is essential to uncover the root causes of issues and break down the truths behind the surface. For instance, I questioned the agenda behind the media's coverage of Hurricane Katrina. Why were these individuals labeled as migrants? What was the underlying motive? It seemed to perpetuate the notion of black people being inferior in this country and justified withholding investments for their recovery.

While some may find this idea disturbing, it is crucial to evaluate the efforts made to rebuild and support the areas affected by Katrina. The displaced individuals faced immense challenges, and the media's focus on portraying them as migrants instead of highlighting their resilience and hope was disheartening.

I chose to pursue magazine article writing as a way to tell deeper stories and challenge the narratives presented by the media. I believe it is essential to question the agendas behind the stories we consume and strive to provide a more accurate and compassionate representation of communities and individuals.

In my gesture to volunteer, my thoughts were, compassion allows us to recognize and respond to the suffering of others. It motivates individuals to take action to alleviate the pain, whether it be providing emotional support, offering a helping hand, or advocating for change. By extending compassion, we can make a positive impact on the lives of those who are facing adversity.

Why can't the media consider incorporating this role or standard, given its proven effectiveness? I acknowledge that people have an appetite for sensational news, and it's understood that they desire it. However, allowing it to overshadow real news is perplexing. We know that people relate to stories that reflect themselves. During the period following the Great Migration, Black individuals not only built wealth in this country but also established newspapers and magazines that celebrated their remarkable achievements. It was only when these communities started to face dismantlement that the media's focus shifted towards violence. To illustrate this change, let's explore Chicago, an area I am well acquainted with and have extensively discussed.

Let's just be honest, in the mid-20th century, crime journalism gained prominence, with newspapers and later television news programs highlighting violent crimes and criminal activities. This shift was influenced by the public's fascination with true crime stories.

Publishing companies were able to profit greatly from the combination of the "War on Drugs" and society's fascination with crime. The area I grew up in, which my mother eventually moved my brother and me away from, deteriorated into a drug- ridden neighborhood plagued by poverty and substance abuse. Families began to fall apart, and we were constantly exposed to stories of death, violence, and incarceration. By the early 1990s, the "War on Drugs" was in full force, but many argue that it failed to truly eradicate the chaos caused by street drugs. Despite these efforts, addiction continues to persist, resulting in over 45 million drug-related arrests.

The underlying cause for both drug dealers and users is the struggle for survival. Numerous experts believe that instead of solely focusing on addiction, we should be examining the reasons behind the immense pain that leads to it, particularly with the introduction of new illegal drugs into the market. Poverty is the ultimate answer to why there is so much pain fueling addiction and drug sales. Certain media organizations have covered the issue of poverty and the decline of once vibrant communities, now destroyed by disinvestment, drug abuse, and violence. The truth is that people living in these dysfunctional environments carry deep trauma, which becomes fodder for headlines and stories.

The narrative that fatherless homes create violent neighborhoods is often perpetuated, despite the fact that, as my story demonstrates, men were actively present in these communities. This part of the story is conveniently omitted. Those who promote this narrative often hold a White supremacist mindset, as they understand that the root cause of fatherless homes is the removal of opportunities that allowed men to flourish, support their families, and build wealth.

Violence has become a widespread public health crisis, and it is no longer a surprising occurrence. The most effective way to address epidemics is through funding and research to determine their root causes and prevent them from happening. However, the media often focuses on the aftermath of violent events rather than the efforts being made to address the underlying issues.

Finding the root cause of many issues is crucial, especially in the field of data surveillance and reporting. Unfortunately, there is often a lack of respect for this work, with people questioning its authenticity and manipulation. However, through analyzing data, trends, and reporting over the years, we can sometimes uncover the underlying reasons behind these issues. Resolving them, however, requires extensive effort, funding, research, and gathering accounts from those affected. Healing wounds in communities, particularly those deeply impacted, can take decades. Nevertheless, data can provide valuable insights into the "why" behind certain problems.

In my work, I was drawn to a project focused on discovering the reasons behind violent deaths, such as homicides and suicides. By narrowing down these factors through data surveillance, we were able to identify mental health issues, proximity challenges, and poverty-related factors. This information became instrumental in securing funding and implementing initiatives to address these issues in the affected communities.

It is essential for journalists and data collectors to collaborate in order to effectively report on the data and its implications. By understanding the trends and narratives derived from police departments and other sources, reporters can relay this information back to the community. However, it is important to acknowledge that human error can still exist in data collection and analysis. Consistency and trends within the data should be evaluated and questioned to gain a deeper understanding of what is happening in communities. It is crucial to engage with community members who have a vested interest in creating positive change and to involve them in the decision-making process.

Building strong communities requires inclusivity and addressing the root causes of issues. By utilizing media as a tool for communication, we can bridge the gap between policymakers, leaders, law enforcement, and the people.

Media plays a significant role in developing communities and creating relationships. It helps navigate complex legalities and legislation, allowing common people to understand and participate in important discussions. It is a powerful instrument that shapes the future and connects generations. It is crucial to use media to connect the dots, establish a firm foundation, and foster growth within our communities. Sensationalism and superficial reporting undermine these efforts and hinder the progress we can achieve together. All of this either get to the root to heal issues or establishes a firm foundation, so if the root is ever exposed you see that it was planted by a community of people who cared.

Former President Obama, in an interview with Anderson Cooper on CNN, emphasized the importance of investing in local media as part of building a legacy. This resonated with me because I strongly believe that the media plays a crucial role in reinvesting in communities.

In an article I wrote for One Purpose Magazine, "Economic Development for Black America," the significance of the Tulsa Star, a Black-owned newspaper, was highlighted. This publication regularly informed African Americans about their legal rights and any court rulings or legislation that affected their community. The first African American periodical, Freedom's Journal, was started by Samuel Cornish and John Brown Russwurm in 1827. Today, some of the prominent black newspapers are the Los Angeles Sentinel, the Chicago Defender, and the Washington Afro. The Chicago Defender, founded in 1905 by Robert S. Abbott, played a leading role in the Great Migration of African Americans from the South to the North.

While sensationalism has been used by newspapers like the Chicago Defender to boost circulation, it is essential for local news to focus on accurate reporting without sacrificing the facts. Sensationalized news may provoke public interest and excitement, but it can compromise accuracy. In our local communities, we cannot afford to lose sight of the facts or overlook important details. There is too much at stake, including voting rights in many areas across the country. Black media outlets play a crucial role in informing communities about how these laws impact them.

It is important to evaluate how local newspapers cover relevant issues that affect your community. Do they exist? Do you support them? Do you regularly check in to stay informed about what's happening locally? Being intentional about seeking out and sharing content from these newspapers is crucial. It is also important to consider the involvement of people of color in these publications, from top to bottom. Additionally, holding local businesses accountable by supporting newspapers that serve your community is essential.

Instead of consuming media that paints a negative picture, we should demand that they focus on what enhances our community. Our interests should drive the narrative.

In the previous chapter, I discussed a student who was known for her aggression and how I was able to connect with her and understand the origins of her behavior. She had a lot to teach me, even though she may not have been aware of it. If someone had acknowledged and articulated her greatness, her life could have taken a different path. Of course, it takes more than one person to make a difference. You need a support system to build you up when so much has been done to tear you down.

The media and education play a significant role in shaping these support systems. Historically, black colleges were established to show black students that they have the potential to succeed. In my own experience attending elementary school in Englewood, Chicago, our education focused on our black heritage. We learned about black history, the contributions of black individuals, and even had schools named after black people. These efforts aimed to demonstrate the possibilities available to us and the importance of having systems in place to support our aspirations.

During my time working at a school with the student I mentioned in this book, I had discussions about her development with the assistant principal, administrator, and teacher. We were preparing for a meeting with her parents and social worker because she was looking to graduate that year. During our classroom meeting, the teacher asked about her career path, but it wasn't mentioned in her paperwork. The teacher didn't know what she wanted to be. I informed them that she expressed interest in becoming a police officer or a writer. However, the administrator simply suggested putting "hair stylist" as her career choice.

This incident made me realize that our educational and support systems should allow students to explore their possibilities without limitations. We shouldn't impose our own perceptions or stereotypes on them. While being a hairstylist is a fantastic career path with significant success in the black community, it wasn't what this student desired. Stereotyping and boxing people based on preconceived notions perpetuates the issues caused by systemic racism. We need to pay more attention to how these systems shape and limit our students' dreams and aspirations.

It is essential to address systemic racism on a smaller scale as well. We often discuss the pipeline to prison in educational programs, which are crucial. However, we also need to consider how we shape our students' experiences and exposure within the school system and classrooms. By providing diverse and inclusive educational environments, we can help break the cycle of perpetuating stereotypes and limited expectations.

In a world fraught with pressing challenges, one crucial concept emerges as a beacon of hope: addressing the roots of problems rather than merely addressing their symptoms.

Picture a paradigm shift where we no longer settle for quick fixes that merely slap a band-aid on deep wounds. Instead, we dare to roll up our sleeves and confront the core of the matter head-on. This transformative approach promises not just temporary relief, but lasting change for the betterment of society at large.

When we devote ourselves solely to treating symptoms, we merely scratch the surface of the issues plaguing us. Such short-sighted measures might momentarily ease discomfort, but they come at an unfathomable cost – a cost that our fragile social fabric cannot afford to bear.

Many urban cities are experiencing this unfortunate reality. These problems have been overlooked for far too long, and the consequences of this neglect are impacting people directly. People are departing from major cities, and they no longer wish to return to offices for work, especially in the wake of the pandemic. The significant urban centers were severely affected as COVID-19 shattered our sense of normalcy. The road to recovery has been arduous because many of these cities are built upon fragile foundations. At the core of all communities lie the people themselves.

In recent times, urban centers across the globe have found themselves at a crossroads, grappling with a series of issues that have been neglected for far too long. These problems, which may have simmered beneath the surface, have now reached a boiling point, demanding our urgent attention.

The consequences of this prolonged avoidance are affecting people in myriad ways. A prominent trend that has emerged is the exodus from major cities. People, once drawn to the bustling streets and towering skyscrapers, are now seeking alternatives. The pandemic played a pivotal role in accelerating this shift. Remote work, necessitated by health concerns, showed us that many jobs could be performed from the comfort of our homes. As a result, the traditional allure of urban living, with its long commutes and high living costs, has lost some of its appeal.

The pandemic's impact on cities was profound. COVID-19 disrupted our daily lives, shuttered businesses, and left an indelible mark on the global economy. The process of rebuilding and returning to normalcy has been an uphill battle, primarily because many cities stand on precarious foundations. Economic disparities, inadequate healthcare systems, and housing challenges have been laid bare, exposing the vulnerabilities that have festered for decades.

We have to remember that at the heart of every community are the people themselves. People form the lifeblood of cities, and their well-being should be the foremost priority. The current urban transformation offers an opportunity for cities to reinvent themselves, to prioritize the needs and aspirations of their residents, and to build more inclusive, sustainable, and resilient communities, as we talk about through this book, with the foundation being compassion.

Despite current struggles, the strength and ingenuity of city inhabitants provides a glimmer of hope. Urban areas have long been sites of advancement and growth, and this crisis may inspire groundbreaking developments. To ensure that cities can withstand this test, the core issues need to be addressed, with resources directed towards infrastructure, cost-effective housing, and equitable chances. With the help of local media, cities have the potential to emerge from this period even more dynamic than before.

The shifts and challenges facing urban cities today are substantial, but they also present an opportunity for meaningful transformation. By recognizing the importance of their people, cities can chart a course toward a brighter, more inclusive future where the allure of urban living is revitalized, and the needs of their diverse communities are met with purpose and determination. Being from Chicago I can't help but be optimistic and hopeful.

Imagine a world where we're smart about how we use our resources. Instead of just tackling the surface-level issues, we dig deep and figure out what's really going on. That's the key to making a real impact. We've gotta understand the root causes and then fix 'em. When we do that, we'll see some serious positive changes in all areas of life. It's all about making things better for everyone!

A counterargument to this is that while understanding the genesis of our challenges is a positive step, it can be a laborious and expensive process. Some may feel the results of this process are not guaranteed and may not lead to any sustainable gains. With that, it may be more effective and efficient to focus our energies on more direct solutions that can be implemented right away and produce tangible results, but I think we've seen enough of this.

Let us, therefore, become impassioned advocates for tackling the roots of problems. Let us commit wholeheartedly to abandoning the futile chase of surface-level symptoms and nurturing sustainable, transformative solutions. In doing so, we not only preserve precious resources, but also carve a brighter, robust, and equitable future for ourselves and generations yet to tread this earth. This cause beckons our unwavering dedication, and it charts a course towards resolute change that we must ardently embrace.

Chapter Three: Fostering a Healthy Society: How to Analyze Data for Reporting

"Data has always been there; we're just the generation that sees its value, for the better."

Compassion isn't just some abstract idea—it's got real benefits for our bodies and minds. You know those times when you've reached out to help someone or shown genuine care? Well, turns out you're not just making their day, you're doing yourself a favor too.

The reality is—compassion has for myself and others the proven ability to dial down stress. I often find myself, when steps focusing on just being kind to others and begin to see a shift

I've read a number of research papers on my personal self healing journey I learned that showing compassion can have positive benefits on your immune system,. Compassion's like its personal trainer, LOL, giving it that extra boost. Studies have even shown that being compassionate gives your immune system a little pep talk, if you will, but you can read about that at another time.

Now, here's the big picture: compassion isn't just about you— it's about building a society where folks look out for each other. Think about it as a ripple effect of goodness. You help someone out, they do the same, and before you know it, we're all living in a world where kindness is king.

Imagine if we all embraced that compassion mindset. Our world would be a place where stress takes a backseat, immune systems stand strong, and people genuinely care for one another. So, don't underestimate the power of compassion—it's not just a concept, it's a way to make our world a better place. Life is a journey marked by experiences, observations, and stories passed down through generations. While I may not have extensive research to bolster my viewpoint, I bring to the table a lifetime of lived encounters within my community. A sense of concern and compassion guides me as I delve into a topic that has long been overlooked—the impact of stress on the black community. Let us embark on this exploration together.

At 40 years old, I stand at a juncture where reflections on the past pave the way for understanding the present. I may not be as young as I once was, but the years behind me have bestowed upon me the ability to assess situations and form opinions. One of these opinions centers around the role of stress within the black community—a concern that, in my estimation, outweighs the attention it has received from researchers.

Looking back at my grandparents and their parents, I can't ignore the fact that they departed from this world prematurely. While medical advancements have extended lifespans, there remains a striking disparity in health outcomes within the black community. It is true that modern medicine has granted us the gift of longer lives, yet it's important to acknowledge that historical health disparities persist. The question then arises: Could stress be the unspoken antagonist?

In conversations with my mother, I am reminded that the concept of age has evolved over time. Aging is not what it used to be; the passage of time carries a different weight now. I observe how the younger generation emphasizes mindfulness when it comes to mental health, a stark contrast to the survival-focused mindset of earlier times. The past generation's struggles often overshadowed the importance of evaluating the toll stress takes on mental well-being.

While some research touches on the topic, there is a distinct absence of studies that truly delve into the intersection of the black experience, premature deaths, and the role of stress. I recently came across an article that left me disheartened. There seems to be a lack of coverage surrounding research on this topic. While certain studies have disappointed me, they have not deterred me from seeking the truth.

A particular study caught my attention, linking premature deaths to the great migration—a period when black families moved from the South to the North in search of better opportunities. This research attributed the increase in premature deaths to heightened tobacco and alcohol use. However, my personal experiences and interactions with research indicate a gap in this reasoning. In my experience, individuals from impoverished backgrounds, much like anyone else, tend to engage in similar habits regardless of financial standing.

It is essential to consider factors that research may have overlooked. While economic improvements were achieved through migration, the emotional toll should not be ignored. The stress and pressure that accompanied these changes led to a different kind of struggle. Despite physical movement, the roots of prejudice and white supremacy persisted, casting a shadow over black lives in the North. The weight of racial tension and societal inequalities persisted, creating a unique blend of stressors that were not adequately captured by existing research.

The challenges didn't end with migration and integration; they continued to evolve. The proximity to predominantly white communities often meant living under a constant cloud of unease. The mere act of commuting to work carried a different weight for black individuals, who faced the pressure of encounters with law enforcement and discriminatory practices. The so-called "war on drugs" further exacerbated the stress and anxieties, echoing the cumulative effect of societal struggles on marginalized communities.

As our society navigates ever-changing legislative landscapes, we find ourselves grappling with uphill battles. The dismantling of affirmative action and other shifts in policies add to the complexities faced by marginalized communities. It's as if one hurdle is cleared only to be replaced by another. The ongoing struggle can be overwhelming, leading to a constant state of oppression that can feel insurmountable.

This brings us to the role of media—a force that holds immense potential for change. It is crucial to move beyond a mere focus on health disparities and begin exploring the contributing factors to premature deaths. The narratives weaved by media should encompass historical contexts, tracing the shifting trends that have shaped the lives of black individuals and communities.

Inclusion becomes our compass, guiding us towards a future where the collective narrative recognizes the shared struggles and triumphs of all communities. By shedding light on the realities that marginalized groups face, media can serve as a catalyst for change, unearthing stories that have long been hidden from view.

It is imperative to remember that compassion and empathy form the core of our actions. The perspective of those directly affected is essential, but it is equally important to hear from those in positions of power and privilege. Their introspection, coupled with awareness, can pave the way for collective solutions that leave no one behind.

Ultimately, this journey towards transformation demands unity and collaboration. As we shine a spotlight on the stressors that underlie disparities, we move closer to a future where equal opportunities are not dictated by zip codes but are shared by all. By embracing these conversations with open hearts and open minds, we forge a path that uplifts every individual and strengthens the bonds of our interconnected communities.

The Power of Data and Stories: A New Era in Journalism

In the ever-evolving landscape of journalism, a hopeful trend emerges, one that resonates with both concern and compassion. As of 2021 and 2022, the field of public health reporting gains momentum, introducing a new facet to newsrooms and media organizations. This development, I believe, represents a significant step forward. In dedicating a reporter solely to public health matters, we open doors to deeper coverage, richer conversations, and a more comprehensive understanding of critical issues.

Imagine having a knowledgeable and dedicated reporter focusing on public health matters—a professional whose mission revolves around bringing these crucial topics to light. This specialized approach brings a host of benefits. First and foremost, it allows for in-depth conversations with experts in the field. By cultivating relationships with these experts, reporters can tap into their knowledge and insights, translating complex information into accessible narratives that inform the public.

A fundamental transformation occurs when this approach is applied to previously overlooked populations. My primary concern with traditional media reporting lies in the inadvertent neglect of communities that conduct extensive research but remain unnoticed. My own experiences while working for a program have highlighted the chasm between these vital researchers and the media. Astonishingly, many of these researchers had never interacted with the media, even within well-known organizations.

It is within this context that I uncovered the paradox— researchers engaged in groundbreaking work, particularly in fields such as preventable injuries, remained largely disconnected from media engagement. This absence of connection underscored a missed opportunity, and it became evident that there was much work to be done in bridging this gap.

Data, as I soon realized, is the unifying thread that runs through all these stories. Researchers, public health organizations, and even law enforcement collect data from various angles, each offering a unique perspective. However, the question lingers— how is this data presented, analyzed, and reported? This query led me to the realization that we are now entering an inclusive era, one that acknowledges the significance of data and the voices it represents.

For me, data reporting became more than just numbers and statistics; it became a way to amplify the voices of those who have been silenced by tragedy. Every data point tells a story—a story of a life lost, a family shattered, and a community impacted. The data, however, does not inherently possess this storytelling power. It is the task of the reporter to unearth these narratives, connecting the dots between data and the human experiences they represent.

This shift in approach is not only about numbers; it's about understanding the circumstances behind each statistic. It's about evaluating the nuances that contribute to preventable deaths. The data reflects health disparities that persist across different communities. This awareness, rooted in data, lays the foundation for the revelation that certain demographics face hurdles that are often invisible on the surface.

Data, quite literally, guides us to confront uncomfortable truths—disparities that exist in healthcare, in trust, in access. It guides us to reflect on the fact that, as a society, we have only just scratched the surface of understanding the intricate web of factors that lead to premature deaths. The data uncovers a world of inequalities that often go unnoticed.

This journey into data has helped us transition from simply reporting the numbers to exploring the narratives beneath them. The numbers, as we have come to realize, are not solely about quantity; they are about stories waiting to be told. This shift in perspective has led us to identify patterns that often hold keys to prevention. The disparities in health outcomes stem from a myriad of factors, and data allows us to trace these patterns and gain insights into possible solutions.

As we delve deeper into this data-driven approach, it becomes clear that inclusion is paramount. Local news organizations can play a significant role by collaborating with researchers who have insights into their communities. These partnerships enable the collection of localized data that is integral to shaping impactful narratives. It is through these stories that we can foster awareness, prevention, and community engagement.

While some might question the validity of anecdotal data, it is imperative to recognize that the narratives of individuals within a community hold immense value. This grassroots perspective adds layers of authenticity to the stories we tell. Combining this with traditional data sources creates a more holistic narrative that resonates with the community's experiences.

Data is a powerful tool, unburdened by bias. It provides an unbiased reflection of reality. While it can be manipulated in certain contexts, the core facts remain unchanged. This foundational truth has the potential to transform narratives, enabling us to uncover the untold stories that lie within every data point.

The emergence of public health reporting as a distinct beat holds the promise of a more comprehensive and inclusive media landscape. By marrying data with storytelling, we weave narratives that are not only informative but also impactful. These narratives possess the potential to drive positive change within our communities, fostering awareness, prevention, and ultimately, a more compassionate society.

Exploring the circumstances behind certain preventable deaths brings us to a sensitive topic: suicide. It serves as an example of how deeply we need to delve into information to truly understand and show compassion. Think of it like diving into data to uncover insights that lead to a more caring perspective. This understanding helps shape the way we talk about and report on suicide.

If we take a closer look, we see that things have changed significantly. Experts in suicide awareness have carefully examined the data to understand how we discuss and present suicide. This has a powerful impact on making these deaths more common among people struggling with specific mental health challenges. By studying this data, they've been able to create awareness campaigns centered around empathy and understanding. This has led journalists and media to approach the topic in a different, more sensitive way.

This effort also aims to break down the negative ideas tied to suicide deaths and how they're talked about. Data plays a crucial role in this. It can't be ignored. If we don't analyze the data to understand the situations that contribute to these deaths, how can we change the way we think?

Society often follows certain standards or ideas set by different groups. When it comes to data, we're now looking at suicide deaths differently. Instead of something to be avoided, we're seeing it as a cause of death. This shift removes the shame people often attach to it. Seeing suicide as a cause of death helps us realize it's tragic nature. This leads to more compassion for the people around the person who died by suicide—the family, friends, and those close to them. They become victims of this tragic event, and we're learning not to overlook them due to the negative associations tied to suicide deaths.

Moreover, we've started to explore the mental health factors that contribute to suicide deaths. This is a very important step in changing our understanding and breaking down the false beliefs. Together, we're reshaping the way we think about and approach this issue with the aim of reducing stigma and promoting compassion.

Understanding difference from personality disorder and mental health, the media has to begin to get very clear on this.

I have dedicated a significant amount of time to self-studying personality disorders and mental health issues. I am concerned that in our reporting, there are instances where we blend these two concepts. I strongly believe that collaborating closely with professionals in our reporting process will assist us in distinguishing between behaviors that might fall within the spectrum of personality disorders and those that could be attributed to mental health issues stemming from the untreated stressors in one's life, as well as how they cope with them.

Some people, especially Black folks, might not realize that the bad experiences they have because of their race can actually cause them to feel stressed and upset inside. They might be really strong and forgiving, which is great, but sometimes these experiences can still affect them.

There was a study that looked at this, and it found that talking about race can be hard for doctors and therapists. This can make it tough for them to help people who are hurting because of racial trauma. And this is a problem because racial trauma can cause feelings that are a lot like something called PTSD, which stands for Post-Traumatic Stress Disorder.

Now, there are also things called "personality disorders." These are ways that some people think, feel, and act that can be different from what's usual. There are different types of these disorders, like when someone feels like they need a lot of attention or when they're really afraid of being alone. Sometimes these ways of thinking and acting can last a long time.

It's important to know that personality disorders are different from mental illnesses. Mental illnesses are health problems that can change how you think, feel, or act. They can make life harder for you, and they can come from different causes.

it difficult to cope with daily life and can often be attributed to chemical imbalances in the brain. Depression, anxiety, schizophrenia, and bipolar disorder are examples of mental illnesses that fall under this category. These conditions often require medical intervention, such as medication or therapy, to help individuals manage their symptoms and improve their overall well-being.

On the other hand, personality disorders are a distinct category within the realm of mental health. Unlike mental illnesses that primarily affect mood, cognition, and behavior, personality disorders specifically relate to enduring patterns of thinking, feeling, and behaving that deviate from cultural norms and cause distress or impairment. These patterns are deeply ingrained and tend to persist throughout a person's life.

Personality disorders are generally grouped into three clusters:

Cluster A Disorders (Odd or Eccentric Behaviors): This cluster includes disorders like paranoid, schizoid, and schizotypal personality disorders. Individuals with these disorders may display peculiar or unusual behaviors, have difficulty forming close relationships, and struggle with social interactions due to their distinctive ways of thinking and perceiving the world.

Cluster B Disorders (Dramatic, Emotional, or Erratic Behaviors): Borderline, narcissistic, histrionic, and antisocial personality disorders belong to this cluster. People with cluster B disorders often have intense and unstable emotions, struggle with impulse control, and exhibit behaviors that can be challenging to manage in both personal and professional settings.

Cluster C Disorders (Anxious or Fearful Behaviors): Avoidant, dependent, and obsessive-compulsive personality disorders fall under this cluster. Individuals with these disorders may experience overwhelming anxiety, fear of rejection, and a strong desire for control and order in their lives. These traits can significantly impact their ability to engage in healthy relationships and adapt to different situations.

It's important to note that diagnosing personality disorders can be complex and requires a thorough assessment by mental health professionals. Effective treatment often involves psychotherapy, particularly dialectical behavior therapy (DBT), cognitive-behavioral therapy (CBT), or schema therapy. Unlike many mental illnesses that can be treated with medication alone, personality disorders typically benefit more from long-term psychotherapeutic approaches that address the underlying patterns of behavior and thought.

While personality disorders and mental illnesses are both part of the broader spectrum of mental health, they have distinct characteristics and necessitate different approaches to diagnosis and treatment. Understanding these differences can help reduce stigma, promote accurate diagnoses, and ensure that individuals receive appropriate care tailored to their specific needs.

I might not be an expert on mental health, but it's my responsibility to learn about these topics if I'm going to write about them. I want to make sure I have the right information so I don't give the wrong ideas to people when I talk about things related to mental health.

One topic that hasn't been explored much is how the media talks about mass shootings. Everyone wants to stop mass shootings from happening, but we also need to figure out how to talk about these complicated issues without creating stigmas. Using accurate facts is really important when we discuss these things.

Mental health is a universal experience. It's an integral part of our lives, woven into the fabric of our existence. Whether we realize it or not, each one of us has a mental health story. It might be our own battle with anxiety, depression, or another mental health condition, or it could be the story of a loved one, a friend, or a colleague. These stories are as diverse as the people who hold them, yet they share a common thread—the undeniable ubiquity of mental health challenges.

In a world where mental health challenges are so prevalent, one would think that discussing them openly and honestly would be the norm. Unfortunately, this is far from the reality. Our society clings to the toxic notion that discussing mental health is taboo, that it's something to be concealed, swept under the rug, and not spoken about in polite company. This silence perpetuates misconceptions and allows confusion to flow through conversations without being properly addressed.

But what is the cost of this silence? The consequences are dire. It perpetuates suffering and despair by isolating those who need help the most. People battling mental health issues often suffer silently, afraid of the judgment and discrimination they might face if they dare to speak out. They hide their pain behind masks, afraid to reach out for fear of being labeled as "weak" or "crazy."

This silence, this stigma, is an insidious force that erodes our communities from within. It strips individuals of their agency and prevents them from seeking the help and support they desperately need. It deepens the chasm of misunderstanding between those who suffer and those who could provide empathy and assistance.

But the truth is, mental health struggles are not a sign of weakness, nor are they something to be ashamed of. They are a natural part of the human experience. Just as we acknowledge when we're physically unwell and seek medical attention, we should also feel comfortable acknowledging when our mental health needs care and support.

Promoting mental health awareness and encouraging open conversations about mental health issues is the key to dismantling this destructive stigma. It's a powerful antidote to ignorance, a light that pierces through the darkness of misunderstanding, and a bridge that connects those who suffer to the help they need.

The benefits of promoting mental health awareness and openness are immeasurable. Lives are saved, relationships are strengthened, and communities become healthier and more resilient. When we encourage open conversations about mental health, we foster a society that values the well-being of all its members and recognizes that mental health is just as important as physical health. This transformation doesn't happen overnight, but by shedding light on the darkness of stigma and utilizing the power of data to guide our efforts, we can create a world where no one suffers in silence, and where everyone knows that help is available, and where we all play a part in supporting one another on the journey to mental well-being.

Data can be used to ensure equitable access to mental health services in a variety of ways. Data can be used to identify populations with higher rates of mental health issues, as well as to understand the disparities in access to mental health services across different communities. This can help to inform policy decisions and funding allocations in order to prioritize the most underserved communities. Data can also be used to track the success of mental health initiatives, and to evaluate the effectiveness of existing programs. This can help to ensure that mental health services are effectively reaching the people who need them most.

Some may say that data can be used to identify populations with higher rates of mental health issues, but it may not be effective in tackling the root causes of mental health issues. Data can be used to track the success of mental health initiatives, but it cannot help to address the systemic issues that lead to inadequate access to mental health services in the first place. Also, data can be used to help inform policy decisions, yet it cannot guarantee that those decisions will be fair and equitable. In order to effectively provide equitable access to mental health services, more must be done to address the systemic issues that lead to disparities in access to mental health care.

Various opinions are needed, they make us better, but data is essential for understanding and addressing challenges. It provides evidence, dispels myths, and shows the extent of the issue. With data, we can evaluate interventions, address disparities, and combat mental health stigma effectively.

Chapter Four: Equality and Inclusion in Media: It Starts at the Top

"Everything has a trickle down effect; why not let what trickles, be good."

When people show compassion, they're basically breaking down walls and making the world a friendlier place. It's like when you're nice to someone, even if they're different from you. That's what compassion is all about – seeing the worth in each person and treating them with respect. And when that happens, it's like a party of fairness and equality.

Think about a puzzle with all these different pieces – different colors and shapes. When you put them together, it makes this amazing picture. Compassion is like that puzzle – it's understanding that every piece (or person) is special. When people get that, they make sure everyone gets the same chances and treats them fairly. It's like making sure everyone gets to play on the playground.

Let's shift to diversity and inclusion. It's kind of like having a favorite type of music, but still respecting other people's jams. Everyone should totally be part of the fun, but sometimes things get a bit tricky. Just like any family, our country has its ups and downs. We're not perfect, but that's okay – we're all figuring things out.

So, even though it's great that everyone should be included, we also need some guidelines to keep things fair. It's like having rules in a game to make sure everyone has a shot. That's why we're talking about it in the earlier chat. We're all working together to make the puzzle of our world fit together just right.

Diversity, equity, and inclusion is a topic that holds deep complexity for me, particularly when it intersects with journalism. This discussion should, in all honesty, be straightforward. The principles of diversity, equity, and inclusion ought to serve as the bedrock of journalism, extending beyond race or ethnicity to encompass all backgrounds and experiences. It's about inclusiveness, whether we're talking about disabilities, unique circumstances, or any other factor that might otherwise lead to exclusion.

In my view, journalism should be a realm where inclusiveness and diversity are fundamental, self-evident aspects. Unfortunately, this hasn't always been the case. Media has, at times, portrayed certain demographic groups in a specific light, shaping narratives that perpetuate unfair stereotypes. One such example is the historical narrative that has been constructed around African-Americans as being lazy, a stereotype that was fueled by media outlets and continues to echo even today.

This narrative has had a lasting impact, despite the tremendous efforts and contributions of Black Americans. The prevailing notion that we must constantly strive to prove these stereotypes wrong underscores the profound effects of media's influence. This extends to the impressive educational achievements of Black women, who often find themselves overexerting to shatter these misleading notions.

Within this context, it becomes increasingly evident that the media landscape requires transformation. The conversations we engage in, the narratives we shape, and the voices we amplify are all guided by those who control the outlets. It's paramount that diversity and inclusion be reflected in these decision-making positions, not just for the sake of diversity but to bring authentic perspectives to the forefront.

This awareness has grown more pronounced, particularly after the tragic killing of George Floyd, which ignited widespread discussions on diversity, equity, and inclusion. While this heightened focus is vital and should be integrated into every sector of society, including media and journalism, there's a balance to be maintained.

My concern arises from the fact that communication specialists, often with journalistic talents, were diverted into the realm of diversity and inclusion as this topic surged in prominence. This shift risked sidelining their primary role, which is to convey effective messages to the public. For journalists who are drawn to communication roles due to the lack of lucrative prospects in journalism, it's important to retain our core mission—serving the public by delivering comprehensible and meaningful messages.

The issue I'm highlighting is not exclusively tied to the media landscape but touches on a broader trend. It emphasizes the need for us to stay true to our calling, especially as journalists who often speak for those who are voiceless. Amidst trends and shifts, our purpose remains unchanged—to keep the public informed, educated, and empowered to make informed decisions.

While I acknowledge the importance of cultivating expertise in diversity, equity, and inclusion, I also hold reservations about the practice of redirecting individuals from their core roles for the sake of organizational optics. This approach can inadvertently detract from the essential work of connecting with and enlightening the public.

In essence, the journey towards genuine diversity, equity, and inclusion must be more than a trend—it must become second nature. It demands that we look past surface-level judgments and stereotypes, forging a natural inclination towards appreciating the unique perspectives that each individual brings to the table. This shift requires an ongoing commitment to unbiased storytelling and open-minded conversations. It's about recognizing that a world colored by diverse experiences is richer, more nuanced, and undeniably authentic.

Not too long ago, I had the privilege of sharing a story about an individual who possesses incredible resilience despite facing significant challenges due to their disability. Reflecting on their journey has reaffirmed the profound reasons behind my commitment to this line of work.

This person's narrative resonated deeply with me, as it vividly highlighted the power of human strength amidst adversity. Their journey hasn't been an easy one; they've experienced homelessness and faced daunting decisions, like choosing to navigate the aftermath of traumatic experiences. Through all of this, they've confronted numerous hurdles and misconceptions that society often places upon them. It's a stark reminder that people can be unfairly judged based on circumstances they find themselves in.

The experience of sharing their story has underlined a crucial truth: inclusivity is paramount when telling the stories of our communities. We must actively embrace narratives from those who are often overlooked or marginalized. Despite our differences, our common pursuit of happiness and contentment binds us together. Whether our life path is one we've chosen or one that has been thrust upon us, we all share the aspiration to care for our loved ones and depart this world in peace.

The encounter with this remarkable individual has taught me that every story has value. Their joy in having their story heard, understood, and shared is a testament to the significance of providing a platform for voices that might otherwise be silenced. I came to recognize them as an equal, someone whose unique experiences and insights deserve acknowledgment. This sense of validation is a powerful force, even when it's not actively sought.

In the course of our conversation, a particular thread stood out— relationships, a topic that was resonating widely at that time. I made it a point to approach this subject without judgment, irrespective of their past experiences. It was important to gather their perspective, their wisdom forged through life's journey. I realized that the advice they offered was not only relatable but also profoundly insightful. It underscored the notion that seeking humanity in our interactions, regardless of differences, can yield remarkable wisdom.

Bringing a human touch to our conversations by seeking advice and insights from those whose life paths might diverge from our own is an exercise in empathy and understanding. It's a way of removing the shadow of shame that often shrouds marginalized voices, allowing them to speak openly and authentically. This shift toward inclusivity gradually dismantles the walls that keep people from sharing their stories, from feeling seen and valued.

Every marginalized group carries the weight of the feelings society imposes upon them, feelings of inadequacy and unworthiness. But by weaving their voices into the fabric of our narratives, we begin to unravel these harmful perceptions. It's a small step toward a more compassionate world, one where stories are shared, heard, and cherished, regardless of the circumstances that gave rise to them.

Sometimes, I think that when you arrive at a point where you realize that you cannot move the needle by working within the established systems, sitting at the table isn't always sufficient to get the job done. You must forge your own path, which is by no means an easy task.

This endeavor takes time, especially when it diverges from the well- trodden path that most individuals in your field or area of focus are accustomed to. It's exceptionally challenging because people will invariably question the merit of your ideas, suggesting alternative approaches by saying, "Why not just do this?" They base this on their own experiences, which have proven effective for them. However, merely because something worked for them and brought them financial reward doesn't inherently contribute to advancing inclusivity. In other words, it doesn't necessarily promote a fair distribution of resources among all individuals, regardless of gender, ethnicity, nationality, and other factors.

Is your work genuinely aligned with this objective? Does your presence alone ensure equitable treatment or value? The reality is that often, you need to diverge from the conventional path to establish your own platform, enabling you to foster that inclusivity or even set a model that benefits people. Such a shift can potentially influence corporations to reevaluate their practices and adopt a more diverse, equitable, and inclusive approach.

Creating lasting change demands more than just being present; it requires a proactive effort to reshape the framework in a way that truly embraces diversity and provides equal opportunities for all.

When I decided to launch my publishing company, I wasn't employed by a publishing firm, but I was engaged in publishing to some extent. I had been working in a similar field for a period of time before transitioning to a staff position. In this role, my responsibilities included creating and distributing booklets for specific meetings. While the department I worked in wasn't directly aligned with my expertise, the work I undertook fell within my domain.

I found this experience significant since it taught me the fundamentals of assembling basic books. These skills have proven valuable as I now manage this process independently. Thus, credit is due to that role, and I always express gratitude for it. I've documented this experience in my other book and discussed it in a mini documentary.

The essence of my point is that this role endowed me with a sense of grace when confronting intricate challenges. Even during moments of discomfort or triggers in the workplace, I recognized the importance of seeking the positive aspects.

The broader perspective often outshines immediate difficulties.

This notion remained consistent as I emphasized the value of grace in the context of a staff support position. It humbled me and reinforced the idea that every life occurrence is instructive. During my tenure in this role, I expressed my aspirations to ascend to an editorial position. However, I was informed that such progression was unlikely due to my staff support classification. This distinction limited my upward mobility, a stance reaffirmed by a conversation with a hiring manager.

To confirm this information, I consulted human resources, and they reiterated the organization's practices. This brought me to evaluate my standing. Despite being actively involved in meetings and discussions, with fair management and structural support, my obstacle centered around personal advancement. The organization's structure was not the issue; it was more about my role and how it correlated with my ambitions.

This realization prompted me to consider stepping away and establishing my venture. This move would allow me to shape my career trajectory as I envisioned. My core identity as a journalist was non-negotiable, even if I took on communication roles for financial stability. Journalism has consistently been my entry into various opportunities, and I knew this was the foundation to build upon.

Although I believe organizations bear a responsibility to foster diversity, I also advocate for individual commitment. Writers and journalists, in particular, must remain loyal to their passions and professional objectives. This principle holds significance across careers, especially in a landscape where content creation is prevalent.

In the realm of journalism, specialization is paramount. Identifying a beat cultivates expertise and establishes one as a reliable voice. While contemporary systems accommodate bloggers, content creators, and podcasters, the unique perspective of a trained journalist is indispensable. A well-defined area of focus grants inclusion in vital discussions, making one an asset in targeted efforts for diversity and representation.

I recognize that our profession was impacted during the surge of interest in diversity and inclusion. Journalists were sought after to contribute to DE&I initiatives due to their strong communication skills, even though formal training had not yet proliferated. This phenomenon concerned me, especially for those who hold journalism dear and aim to preserve its role in society. Therefore, while financial stability is attainable through various avenues, upholding the essence of journalism remains paramount.

I wish to emphasize that maintaining passion and purpose in one's career is crucial. In the face of popular trends and shifts, staying true to one's journalistic roots is essential. This reflection is not intended to be a comprehensive guide to shaping careers but rather a recognition of the challenges we face in the diverse and ever-evolving landscape of journalism.

In discussing inclusivity, throughout this entire book, you can observe my strong emphasis on its importance. Almost every chapter delves into the topic of inclusivity. In journalism, inclusivity holds various meanings, particularly concerning content creation, production, and publishing.

Inclusivity, also touches upon themes such as racial and ethnic diversity, women's empowerment, disability awareness, cultural exchanges, mental health representation, and breaking barriers for marginalized individuals. Moreover, it covers subjects like age diversity, LGBTQ+ representation, inclusive advertising, social justice documentaries, and children's media representation. There's a wealth of content to explore when it comes to creating inclusive materials.

As I embarked on my journalism journey, distinct from broadcasting, I re-entered the field after a hiatus and turned to magazine article writing. During this time, I enrolled in an elective course titled "entertainment reporting." Initially, I expected this course to be straightforward, as I held minimal interest in entertainment. However, my history of maintaining a form of social consciousness influenced my perspective. Initially, delving into entertainment didn't strike me as particularly appealing. That changed when I attended the class and engaged with the professor's perspective.

This instructor, a seasoned journalist with Chicago Tribune experience, guided us through challenges stemming from my prior education in the Chicago public school system. My entrance into college left me feeling somewhat disadvantaged due to perceived gaps in the quality of education. The initial years proved arduous, and I diligently worked to bridge these gaps through additional efforts such as utilizing the writing center and attending grammar classes. These challenges persisted as I entered the entertainment reporting class.

Nonetheless, my professor subtly communicated the value of my unique voice. He underscored the significance of mastering foundational skills while retaining my personal tone in writing. This affirmation marked a turning point for me, offering a sense of relief and validation in a journey that often felt like an uphill battle.

Another profound lesson from the class concerned my perception of entertainment reporting. Initially, I associated it with sensationalism and gossip, which was largely influenced by mainstream media portrayals. This perspective shifted as I was introduced to theater and stand-up comedy, which were largely foreign to me due to limited exposure. Our professor stressed that quality journalism involves transitioning from news consumers to news creators. He highlighted the importance of recognizing local interests and niche topics as equally important in preserving journalistic integrity.

A transformative experience took place during a visit to Zanies comedy club, a departure from my usual surroundings. Here I am, driving into the parking lot of Columbia College Chicago, right in the heart of the South Loop between Congress Parkway and Wabash. I pull into the parking lot on this cold, dark night. I used to take evening classes because I was a mom and a full-time student. On top of that, I worked part-time as a bank teller.

I park my silver Dodge Neon under the yellow-painted ill bridge. As I step out of the car, I'm filled with a mix of nervousness and excitement. It's my first time taking one of those L trains. I've never embarked on such an adventure alone before, despite growing up in Chicago. I might have ridden the L as a kid, but I can't recall the experience. As an adult, this is a new journey for me.

I make my way into the building, dressed in my blue ballerina-style flats, jeans, a white leather jacket, and probably a crew-neck sweater underneath, with a scarf tied around my neck for the chilly Chicago weather. I sit down in class, and the teacher explains the plan. He's clearly enthusiastic about introducing us to the world of journalism through comedy.

After the briefing, I find myself hesitating. I'm at the back of the group, still thinking about my car parked in the lot. I consider just driving instead, but I don't know my way around the city well. Plus, I didn't print out MapQuest directions since GPS systems weren't as common back then.

Nonetheless, I decide to continue. The teacher kindly covers our onboarding expenses, including train fares. Some of the students have U-Passes, and most of us use those. We all ride the trains with our U-Passes, and I'm grateful I didn't have to pay.

We board the train, likely the pink line, and I start learning about the various colors and lines of the L system. My classmates are intrigued by the fact that I've never been on an L train before, even though I'm from Chicago. It becomes a topic of conversation, and I realize how unusual my experience is for them.

The train ride turns out to be less eventful than expected. It's not the big deal I thought it might be. We exit the train near the Zanies building, and my youthful uncertainty kicks in. I'm around 22 years old, but I'm still wondering if I'm old enough to enter the comedy club. I'm used to being a young mom, not a club-goer.

We enter the club, and some of the older students order cocktails while there's a two-drink minimum. I settle for a Sprite or soda. The comedy show begins, and I recognize the first comedian. Despite my familiarity with more mainstream comedians, the style and atmosphere of this show are different. It's cleaner, and the focus isn't solely on my ethnicity.

As the headliner takes the stage, I'm thrilled. This comedian is from a TV show or movie that I can't recall at the moment. It's a new perspective on comedy, not tied to a particular culture. The atmosphere is inclusive and diverse, unlike what I'm used to. It's a unique experience that challenges my preconceptions about comedy.

In the end, I realize that this adventure, though initially nerve-wracking, was a valuable and eye-opening journey. It showed me a different side of comedy and exposed me to new perspectives.

This excursion introduced me to comics from diverse background, genders, and identities. Assigned with the task of narrating their stories, I grasped the significance of inclusivity in storytelling. By immersing myself in their narratives and shedding personal biases, I aptly captured their perspectives. Entertainment reporting evolved into a tool for bridging divides and fostering understanding between disparate communities.

Entertainment for a lot of people isn't what's happening in Hollywood, so I talk about this being inclusive content. We took a trip to Zanie's Comedy Club, which was completely outside of where I was typically be or hang out. It was north of River North and I was in the South Loop of Chicago at college. It was very different because I was introduced to people that were not in my community, but I was challenged to tell the stories of these comics who had completely different backgrounds. Even their work was different from what I was used to. They traveled from place to place, had different nationalities, genders, and some were part of the LGBTQ community. It was just a melting pot of different backgrounds in this comedy room. I had to tell their truth and talk about their comedy with my background. I learned that entertainment reporting can be a great tool to provide inclusivity and to make people feel like they are getting to know individuals that are not typically in their atmosphere of influence. I also realized that comedy rooms are safe environments and that I could go alone and make friends. There was no judgment and people welcomed me into their tables. It is important to find these niche markets where we can have these experiences of different cultures and people with different layers and include that in our content, so that we can expand and explore different ideologies and make experiences outside of our own environment normal.

Attending comedy rooms also illuminated their welcoming and secure environment, enabling independent connections with people. These spaces exemplified microcosms of inclusivity, where I could engage with others and broaden my horizons. The lesson underscored that inclusivity extends beyond broad social justice discussions; it encompasses representing various cultures, ideologies, and experiences.

My journey from dismissing entertainment reporting to recognizing its potential for inclusivity was transformative. It taught me that inclusivity thrives not only in grand narratives but also in the subtleties of diverse cultures and experiences. Through my writing, I endeavor to normalize and amplify voices that deviate from the norm, rendering unfamiliar experiences relatable to a broader audience.

In my writing, I am driven by a profound commitment to transcending the limitations that often divide us as individuals and communities. It is my steadfast purpose to dismantle the barriers of understanding and foster a climate of empathy and inclusivity. Through my literary endeavors, I seek to champion and magnify voices that are frequently marginalized or overlooked, appreciating the tremendous richness and depth inherent in the diverse human experience.

In a world too often dominated by prevailing narratives that reinforce societal norms and perpetuate conformity, it becomes imperative to acknowledge and celebrate the myriad of perspectives that exist. Each individual possesses a unique story, a tapestry of personal encounters and beliefs that contribute to the shaping of their identity and worldview. These stories, often obscured and subjugated, encapsulate the very essence of our human condition with unparalleled depth and vibrancy.

When I speak of normalizing these voices, it is an endeavor to challenge the stigma and biased judgments that historically burden those whose experiences deviate from the established "norms." I strive to disrupt the silence that has traditionally enveloped these narratives, rendering them invisible and unheard. By exposing these distinctive stories to the light, I aim to illuminate their beauty and the undeniable truth that they are not deviations, but indispensable threads in the intricate fabric of our collective human existence.

It is my dedication to amplify these voices, enabling them to resonate powerfully within the broader consciousness. By skillfully weaving these stories through the artistry of language, my intention is to augment their impact, connecting them with a diverse range of readers. I firmly believe that these narratives possess the capacity to move hearts, challenge preconceived notions, and inspire transformative change. They bear witness to the resilience, courage, and inventive spirit of those who have traversed unique life paths.

By rendering the unfamiliar more accessible, I endeavor to bridge the divide between "us" and "them," forging connections and fostering deeper empathy. In transforming the enigmatic into the familiar and the unexplored into the understood, my writing creates a space where individuals from all walks of life can recognize a fragment of their own experiences within the narratives of others. Through this sense of shared experience, we can discover our common humanity and transcend the limitations of our differences.

In a world sometimes fractured by division, my purposeful prose champions diversity and exalts the extraordinary stories that shape us. It serves as a compelling reminder that within the unconventional lie beauty, within the marginalized lie strength, and within the unspoken lie profound truths yet to be uncovered. My words are an impassioned rallying cry, inviting readers to embark upon a journey of exploration into the vast tapestry of human existence, to actively listen to the silenced voices, and to ultimately acknowledge that, despite our disparities, we are all irrevocably interconnected in the grand narrative of life.

Chapter Five: Amplifying All Voices: Not Creating the Narrative, but Establishing it

Imagine you're strolling through a vibrant garden filled with all sorts of flowers. Some of these flowers are tall and bold, soaking up plenty of sunlight, while others are smaller and tucked away in the shade. Amplifying voices is like carefully tending to those hidden flowers so they can bloom just as brilliantly as the rest.

Think about a garden with rare, flowers. These flowers might not catch your eye at first glance, but when you take the time to notice them, they're breathtaking. Amplifying voices is like taking a moment to appreciate those hidden beauties and share their uniqueness with others.

Now, consider a garden party with a variety of dishes on the buffet table. Some dishes might be front and center, getting all the attention, while others are nestled in the background. Amplifying voices is like making sure those background dishes are highlighted too. By doing that, you're adding diversity and flavor to the spread.

In the world of communication, amplifying voices is like giving a quiet, thoughtful friend a chance to speak up. It's about asking them, "What do you think?" and valuing their perspective. Just like a garden needs different types of plants to thrive, society flourishes when all voices are heard.

So, in the garden of life, amplifying voices is about nurturing those hidden flowers, savoring the unique flavors, and creating a space where every voice can bloom and contribute to the rich tapestry of our world.

The concept of amplifying voices truly gained traction after the tragic murder of George Floyd in 2020. At that time, a multitude of individuals who had previously felt voiceless saw an opportunity to express themselves and have their contributions to society acknowledged. This sentiment was evident across various domains. In an earlier section of this book, I discussed researchers who had been marginalized by the media. Even during the period of amplifying voices, I observed momentum growing within this sector as they sought recognition amidst the pandemic and the widespread turmoil gripping the nation.

In such a critical period, many individuals driven by the desire to help people were eager for their voices to be heard. The uncertainty surrounding civil rights, combined with the confusion, dysfunction, and chaos of the time, left us unsure whether we would emerge from these challenges. During this phase, everyone sought to align themselves with the right side of history, aiming for their viewpoints to be acknowledged. This collective desire aimed to demonstrate care for both the nation and its people, regardless of their societal roles or positions.

Amidst the multifaceted tests faced by society, using one's voice became paramount. The significance of amplifying voices may have waned slightly since then, marking that specific era. Nevertheless, it still remains relevant as people from all walks of life continue to require a platform to express themselves in order to foster equality. I previously touched on how my occupation provided a pathway for me to champion the voiceless. To me, this involved identifying circumstances that perpetuated disparities and raising awareness to prevent their recurrence.

When I consider the term "amplify," especially in the context of journalism and the media, I envision making voices more impactful, resonant, and attention-grabbing. However, my aspiration, particularly as a woman and as part of the African- American experience in this country, extends beyond mere volume or exaggeration. What I genuinely yearn for is the recognition of my voice and experiences as equally valuable contributions within this nation. This entails viewing them on par with anyone else's.

There exists a prevailing notion that we must be outspoken, projecting a specific attitude to ensure our voices are acknowledged, particularly when we strive to be part of key conversations or environments. While the adage of "sitting at the table" holds true, our ultimate aim is for our voices to hold value in these settings. Although the phrasing may not be as catchy as "amplified voices," the core essence underscores the importance of recognition. Throughout my own experiences, I have been fortunate to collaborate with individuals who regard my perspective as an invaluable input to decision-making processes.

This facet holds immense significance in elevating and amplifying voices – acknowledging them as essential viewpoints to be considered. This principle resonates deeply within our communities, where media plays a pivotal role. Media has the potential to provide a voice to those whose experiences are typically marginalized, utilizing these narratives to affect change within legislative bodies and various levels of leadership.

By amplifying these voices, by making them more prominent and resonant, we inherently assign them greater importance, mirroring the adage that the squeaky wheel receives attention. However, there's a need to distinguish between loudness and significance; sometimes, individuals are compelled to be louder to ensure they are taken seriously. For me personally, introspection reveals that while I am generally reserved and observant, I am not typically loud. This could be attributed to past insecurities or lack of confidence, although this no longer holds true.

My inclination to listen and my visionary thinking are prominent traits. Yet, due to my quieter nature, my ideas have often gone unnoticed. Strangely, it's when more vociferous voices fail that my concepts are reconsidered. I've pondered whether adopting a louder demeanor could lead to more recognition, though it's unfortunate that this dynamic persists due to learned behaviors and societal norms.

Amplifying voices signifies more than sheer volume; it encapsulates valuing and recognizing the worth of these expressions. It involves taking concrete actions based on this valuation.

Let's think about that for a moment, "It involves taking concrete actions based on this valuation."

Now, take a moment to ponder this scenario: Imagine being a dedicated contributor to your community, a homeowner who frequents local businesses, and an individual who calls this place home. You're a part of the very fabric of your community, and you consider your neighbors as an extended family. You're there, day in and day out, witnessing the world around you evolve and change. However, as time goes by, you start to notice something unsettling. You're never invited to the decision-making table. Your input is never sought, and you're not even welcome at the meetings where crucial matters are discussed. Even if you decide to attend these gatherings on your own initiative, you're met with a cold shoulder and a palpable lack of inclusion.

These microaggressions and subtle slights begin to accumulate, eroding your sense of belonging. They send a clear message to someone whose voice remains unheard: "You don't really matter." This is not the message we should be sending to anyone in our community. Every individual should feel valued and invested in their community, irrespective of their background or identity. It goes beyond mere financial contributions; it's about shaping and nurturing the very essence of the community.

When you're a part of a community, you should have the power to influence its direction. This power extends beyond the monetary contributions; it's about shaping the community's culture, priorities, and future. However, when you find yourself perpetually locked in battles just to prove that your voice deserves to be heard, it becomes exhausting. You're fighting for a seat at the table, not for personal gain, but to create an environment where your children can thrive.

One of the fundamental reasons we come together in communities is to collaborate, to pool our collective wisdom and resources for the betterment of all. The idea is that everyone contributes their unique perspective and experiences, enriching the collective decision-making process. No one should be ostracized or left on the fringes. Every voice in the community should be heard and amplified through genuine inclusion and participation.

We must recognize that community is not just a place; it's a dynamic, living entity shaped by its members. It's imperative that we acknowledge and embrace the concept that a community transcends mere geography; it's a vibrant, living entity molded by the collective efforts and experiences of its members. In essence, a community is not confined to a physical location but is a dynamic tapestry woven from the diverse threads of its residents' lives, stories, and perspectives. Within this intricate tapestry, every single member's voice deserves to be heard and valued.

A community is more than just the sum of its buildings, streets, and parks. It's the shared history, aspirations, and challenges of its people that give it life and character. Each member contributes a unique hue to the collective canvas, painting a rich portrait of what the community represents. These contributions are not limited to financial or material aspects; they extend to the thoughts, ideas, and dreams of every individual who calls that community home.

In this living entity we call a community, the voice of each member carries significance. It's not merely a formality or token gesture to include diverse perspectives; it's a fundamental principle that underpins the vitality and resilience of the community. When we recognize that every voice is a thread in the tapestry, we foster an environment where people feel not only heard but also empowered to actively participate in shaping their community's present and future.

This inclusive approach to community building goes beyond a superficial recognition of diversity; it celebrates it. It understands that the collective strength of a community is not derived from conformity but from the harmonious interplay of distinct voices. By ensuring that every voice is not only acknowledged but actively sought out, we create a space where innovation, empathy, and collaboration thrive.

In such a community, residents feel a deep sense of belonging and purpose. They recognize that their unique experiences and insights contribute to a mosaic of ideas that can address challenges, drive positive change, and enhance the overall well-being of the community. Moreover, they understand that diversity is not a source of division but a wellspring of resilience, adaptability, and creativity.

A community is far more than a physical location; it's a living, breathing entity shaped by its members. To unlock its true potential and vitality, we must honor the voices of all its constituents. By doing so, we create a community where every member feels valued, heard, and empowered, ultimately leading to a stronger, more vibrant, and inclusive collective that benefits everyone.

When we find value in our voices we find the find in supporting local media, because then we get the relevance of the process and desire to invest in it.

And, funding is a crucial aspect that strongly influences the work of independent journalists like us or those who are starting their own media platforms. Think of funding as the money that helps us do what we do – whether it's writing news articles, creating videos, or running a website. It's like the fuel that keeps our journalism engine running.

The interesting thing is that funding isn't just about having enough money to do our work. It's also about where that money comes from and how it can shape what we do. Imagine you want to create a magazine or a website to share news and stories that matter to people. You need money to build your website, pay your writers, and promote your work so that people can find it.

Now, sometimes big companies or advertisers want to help us out by giving us money. They might want to show their ads on our website or in our magazine. This can be a good thing because their money can help us do more and reach more people. But there's a catch – when we take money from these companies, they might expect something in return.

This is where things get tricky. These companies might want us to write about certain topics or in a certain way that makes them look good. They might want to control what we say or how we say it. And suddenly, our journalism isn't just about telling stories that matter – it's about pleasing the companies that give us money.

It's like if you were playing a game and someone gave you a bunch of points to play. But then, they tell you which moves to make and how to play. It's not really your game anymore; it's theirs.

Now, I know we're not here to talk only about money. But it's important to understand how it affects us because it can change what we do and how we do it. That's why I believe it's a good idea to have a clear plan for how we write and share news. This plan helps us stay true to our mission and make sure we don't let money get in the way of telling the truth.

Imagine you live in a city, and you're really good at writing. You start a website where you write about things that matter to your community. People start reading your articles and sharing them because they can relate to what you're saying. You're proud of the work you're doing, and you're making a difference by bringing attention to important issues.

But as your website grows, you start needing more money. You might want to hire more writers or improve your website. This is when you might consider getting money from ads or asking people to subscribe to support your work.

However, getting more money can be tricky too. Some people might offer you money but also want you to write what they want. It's like if someone gave you money to buy a new toy, but then they told you which toy to buy. It's not really your choice anymore.

You might also think about growing your website even bigger, like getting an office or hiring a team. But to do that, you need even more money. This is where things can get really complicated. To get more money, you might need to get more ads or have more people subscribe to your website. And sometimes, to get those ads or subscribers, you have to do things a certain way.

But here's the thing – asking for more money can come with a price. It might mean that you have to change the way you write or the things you talk about. And this can be a problem because you started this journey to tell stories that matter and give a voice to people who might not be heard otherwise.

This challenge is something that a lot of independent journalists face, especially in big cities where the media is a big business. It's not easy to change the way things work when everyone is used to doing things a certain way.

But here's the exciting part: even though it's hard, independent media can still make a big impact. You might not have as much money as big news companies, but you have something even more valuable – a strong connection with your community.

By focusing on stories that matter to your community and staying true to your values, you can create something special. You can show people that news is more than just headlines – it's about sharing stories that make a difference. And when people see that you're genuine and not just trying to make money, they'll trust you more.

So, it's okay to want to grow and make money, but always remember why you started. You wanted to tell stories that matter and give people a voice. Even if it takes longer or feels like a slow process, sticking to your mission is what will truly change things with your stories. And that's a pretty amazing thing to do.

Having said that, it is important to establish a formula and method of writing that ensures a clear understanding and maintains boundaries. The business of serving the people should always take precedence over personal financial gain. When embarking on the journey of starting an independent publication, it may begin with limited resources. Piecing things together, applying for grants, and managing a tight budget is often necessary. However, there comes a point when scaling and growth are desired.

So in essence, scaling up a publication requires more money, potential ad revenue, and reaching a larger audience. It may involve hiring a team, securing a location, and conducting interviews and discussions. While seeking funding and support seems like a logical step, it can be challenging to maintain the original mission and values. Often, when outside organizations provide mentorship and funding, they may also impose their own criteria and standards. This can inadvertently lead to the adoption of patterns and practices that were initially avoided.

I know this may seem redundant, this is a common challenge faced by many independent journalists and media platforms, especially in big cities like Chicago. The media industry in such cities is well-established, and changing its trajectory requires significant effort. However, I believe that independent media can start from the outside and gradually influence the existing narrative. Niche papers, newsletters, and white papers focusing on specific ideas and community growth can make a difference. By producing relevant content and engaging with the community, these platforms can slowly establish a new narrative that is inclusive, equitable, and unbiased.

While there is a temptation to grow rapidly and gain profitability, it is crucial to prioritize the service of the people and the mission of journalism. Building trust and ensuring truth and transparency should be the ultimate goal. Impactful journalism happens when it touches people's lives and communicates with them effectively. This can be achieved by prioritizing meaningful stories and amplifying the voices of those who are often unheard. Each article, publication, or production contributes to changing the narrative and making a lasting impact on society.

Patience is key in this process, as rushing to gain profitability may compromise the authenticity and purpose of our work. Journalism is about more than sensationalism and chasing numbers; it is about making a real difference in people's lives. We should be willing to listen to the experiences of others while being courageous enough to chart our own course. Every experience and circumstance, whether successful or not, adds value and helps shape our journalism missions.

Therefore, when establishing a narrative, it is important to learn from past experiences and use them to guide our direction. We should learn from those who have experience without dismissing their knowledge outright. By adding value to our content and staying true to our mission, we can create impactful journalism, especially if we are independent journalists.

You might have noticed that I often use the phrase "establish the narrative." I prefer "establish" over "create." Let me explain why. When I think of "create," I imagine bringing something entirely new into existence. However, the narrative already exists—it just hasn't been properly told.

The narratives we encounter have been formed through various lenses: people's biases, perceptions, even their micro-aggressions and prejudices. That's how these narratives have taken shape. This is why I prefer to say "establish the narrative." My intention is to build a strong foundation around the realities we face, without creating an idealized version for others.

I want to avoid reshaping reality to fit a particular story, but rather, establish some boundaries that ensure the story remains within fair, balanced, and just limits. I want the voices of those living these realities to be amplified. This way, we can adhere to the truth, the data, the vital aspects, without straying towards sensationalism for attention.

For independent journalists, storytellers, and those invested in their communities, this boundary-setting is crucial. It's not about drawing a vague line; it's about having a clear agenda—to serve the people. When your stories are genuinely in service, there's no room to stray for the sake of creativity alone. While creativity is important, tackling societal issues often requires narratives rooted in facts, experiences, occurrences, data, and the history that shaped them.

All these components help us understand and fuel our drive for change. We need to stay grounded in truth, embracing both the good and the bad aspects. We need to understand how these narratives emerged and the history behind them. This understanding is what motivates us to create positive change.

Disconnecting from reality isn't an option. Our role as journalists, as storytellers, is to contribute to a better world. To achieve that, we must be connected—by establishing narratives that accurately reflect our shared realities

Chapter Six: Teaching Media Literacy in Secondary Education: Equipping Students

When it comes to media literacy, I admire and appreciate the efforts made by the state of Illinois in integrating media literacy into secondary education. This holds great importance to me because I believe that around eighth grade, individuals begin to grasp the workings of legislation and the significance of civic engagement.

A crucial part of civic engagement involves comprehending the media's role in informing individuals about how they can participate and take action. It raises questions about the available information, existing legislation, ongoing leadership efforts, and the community's vested interests. As I discussed earlier, this connectivity is vital, and effective communication holds significance in every facet of life. Thus, incorporating media literacy into the secondary educational curriculum seems prudent. This is the stage where one learns to be a contributing member of a community, to value and participate in the ongoing events, whether it's by embracing sports, joining various groups like speech teams or chess clubs – it's all about community involvement.

In my view, learning media literacy encompasses more than simply differentiating between what's real and what's fake or factual. While that's a component, it doesn't end there because people tend to believe what aligns with their preconceptions. I don't believe journalism can radically change people's beliefs, but I do think that we can instill a sense of journalistic integrity within the communities we invest in.

This is crucial as it establishes a framework within which we can operate. While systems may falter, we shouldn't shy away from reshaping them, particularly for the succeeding generations to have a broader perspective of what our communities should encompass and represent.

When children are taught media literacy, it essentially means fostering engagement through media as a means of community communication. For me, as a journalist, this is a victory because I perceive journalism as a credible resource our community can utilize. It's already ingrained in the constitution, offering a foundation that we can build upon.

I'm going to discuss a somewhat taboo topic for those involved, as this issue carries some sensitivity. I believe this handling of an important matter has caused significant hurt. Sometimes, when we undergo the process of losing something we had deep belief in and invested ourselves into, it becomes difficult to comprehend its necessity or the lack of fault on our part, especially when it concerns a community that we should be nurturing within the media realm.

This applies particularly to young individuals. Taking something away from them seems somewhat cold. I had the opportunity to participate in a program affiliated with my college, where the objective was to mold the upcoming generation of journalists. The individuals involved had substantial stakes in journalism; many had written for major publications and actively influenced the shifts occurring in news organizations, particularly during the advent of the internet and social media. Most of us had a history within the realm of journalism, whether through our academic pursuits or professional endeavors.

The program revolved around individuals who possessed a genuine passion for the art of journalism and the craft of presenting news stories in an inclusive manner. I was invited to join this program as a mentor to the students. This was a humbling experience for me, given that I hadn't remained deeply engaged in mainstream or well-known publications immediately after college. I embarked on my own venture – the creation of a magazine, a long-held aspiration of mine. As such, I hadn't spent time at a prominent publication's editorial table, even though I hailed from a city known for its significant black publications like Ebony and Jet. I never worked with them or earned a place in their newsrooms.

Thus, I felt a profound sense of humility when they considered me capable of guiding these teenagers. The program aimed to build something substantial for the youth in the Chicago area, which was and remains a remarkable feat considering that creating job opportunities for young individuals was not a prevailing conversation at the time. The funding and the ability to garner industry professionals as mentors, coupled with providing stipends as tokens of appreciation for their time, marked this program as invaluable.

Moreover, the structure of the program and the caliber of individuals involved were equally priceless. It tapped into students who exhibited a genuine interest in the field of journalism, a feat made all the more impressive in the era of mainstream influence through social media and the varied digital platforms that capture the attention of youngsters. Considering that journalism doesn't often align with the glitz and glamour seen in the lives of celebrities, it's commendable that these students perceived it as a potential career path. Local news reporters, the true representatives of journalism, are rarely wealthy, which doesn't make the profession alluring.

Yet, it was fascinating to witness the strong desire these young individuals harbored to represent their communities, to tell their stories, and to become the media's voice within their localities. Initially, when I began my journey within this program, I saw it as an exceptionally brilliant idea. The passionate commitment of those involved was palpable; they believed in their work, their skills, and their talents. Being in their presence, you could feel the dedication, passion, and love they poured into their work, which they were eager to pass down to the younger generation.

During my mentor sessions, the ardor and zeal for our craft would overflow, igniting a fire within the youth. This demonstrated to me that they too felt a sense of purpose, recognizing that journalism offered something beyond financial rewards – a stake in their communities, a voice to amplify unheard narratives, and an avenue to serve as a community stakeholder. I remember one student, initially apprehensive about venturing into journalism due to insecurities stemming from transitioning to a diverse environment. However, as she delved into subjects that held personal significance, and as she raised her voice about issues resonating within her community, she discovered her strengths.

Her essay delved into the topic of colorism, which was not extensively addressed at the time. Through her research, interviews, and introspection, she realized that colorism was not only impacting those around her but had also influenced her personal experiences. It was remarkable to witness her growth within such a short span, as mentoring her provided me the privilege of witnessing the transformation facilitated by finding one's niche and using it to spark change.

This experience reaffirmed the importance of connecting the dots for young individuals, showing them how their interests can shape a fulfilling career. Such engagement of youth through projects and programs is vital, as these endeavors fuel their enthusiasm. Incorporating media literacy into education is essential, much like music programs in inner-city schools, although such initiatives are often dwindling. My own high school offered media programs – radio, TV, and even a newspaper – experiences that not all schools can provide today, which is disheartening.

I had mentored for this program for about four years across various sessions, up until it ended abruptly. There were sessions for fall, spring, summer, and winter. I worked intermittently throughout those four years in different sessions. During a period when I was a mentor for the program, I was also a paraprofessional at the high school where I worked.

During this time, I was able to refer a student from the high school to the program. She was accepted and joined. When I met her, I was struck by her charisma and insightful perspectives despite her age. It seemed important to amplify her voice, especially given our discussion about amplifying voices in the previous chapter.

I assisted her with the application process as she was nervous. I guided her to be honest and transparent about her experiences and goals for the program. I should note that our high school was located in the south suburbs, whereas the mentoring program was in downtown Chicago—an urban area distinct from its surrounding suburbs. This made it a significant experience for her to be part of such a renowned institution in the heart of the city.

Her anxiety was understandable as she applied and later went for an interview. I provided support throughout, encouraging her to overcome her fears and complete the process. Not surprisingly, she was accepted into the program, a decision that aligned with my belief that she was an ideal candidate due to my extensive involvement and understanding of their selection criteria.

I felt immense pride in her acceptance and her decision to confront her apprehensions. She navigated the interview process successfully. Although she wasn't assigned as one of my mentees in the program, I observed her mentor speak highly of her. This wasn't unexpected, given my perception of her potential. I must mention that the teachers at her high school held a different view of her, often considering her a troublemaker. However, my impression of her was different. I saw a person with unexpressed thoughts and feelings, searching for a platform to share them.

Upon entering the program, she not only found her voice but also used it to advocate for foster children. She interviewed peers who had similar experiences growing up in the foster care system. Her ability to give voice to those with similar stories was a remarkable demonstration of her character. Her actions stood in contrast to the judgments passed on her by some at her high school. She embraced the opportunity I had suggested and passed it forward, providing a chance for someone else to amplify their voice. In doing so, she became a representative for marginalized foster children —a community often overlooked.

Throughout the program, she excelled. Even beyond her time in the program, I remember that she was frequently highlighted during introductory meetings for new program participants. Her accomplishments were celebrated, not just in her writing but also in her reporting. She effectively utilized various mediums available to young journalists at the time. This was a significant achievement, showcasing the potential of youth in journalism and storytelling. These endeavors aimed to bring understanding and compassion to their experiences, fostering empathy and connection, especially when their stories differ from our own.

That's precisely the path I followed upon entering Journalism school. The very advice I now offer, I had to heed myself – I needed to step out of my comfort zone and take action. Armed with nothing more than a steno pad and a pen, I ventured out to engage in conversations, conduct interviews, and break down barriers.

This experience not only granted me the courage to overcome personal obstacles but also honed my skills as a journalist. Understanding the essence of a journalist's role is crucial if we aim to promote media literacy. While not every profession can be learned by doing the job itself, gaining firsthand experience from a journalist's perspective is invaluable.

I acknowledge that not every educational endeavor can mirror this approach. Naturally, you wouldn't send a student to perform police work when teaching them about law enforcement. However, exposing students to the practical aspects of a profession can significantly benefit their development.

This approach extends beyond the classroom and has a profound impact on personal growth and resilience. My aspirations to become a journalist were born in high school when I visited a new studio and had the chance to meet broadcaster Art Norman. His question to the students about our career aspirations left a lasting impression on me.

In that moment, I was captivated by the studio environment, the bright lights, makeup artists, and the industrious people behind the scenes. I didn't anticipate his question when it reached me, but I blurted out, "I want to anchor the news." His laughter didn't discourage me. Instead, it instilled a desire to ground myself in my work and remain resolute in my pursuits.

Reflecting on that moment, I realized the importance of gradually gaining experience. It is vital for young people to explore a variety of experiences before making career decisions. This exploration helps tailor their skills, interests, and future path. My journey led me into journalism, a path you might be familiar with by now.

However, I faced another challenge in school – my reluctance to approach and converse with people without feeling insecure. To overcome this obstacle, I enrolled in an intriguing class called the "Art of Interviewing." Although it was outside the journalism department, it focused on the Library of Congress Veterans' History Project.

The class tasked us with interviewing veterans from various wars in the United States, a daunting prospect given the depth and trauma involved in their experiences. These interviews required a 90-minute commitment and a series of thoughtfully crafted questions that covered their backgrounds, experiences, goals, and the challenges of returning home after war.

Interviewing my former neighbor, a World War II veteran, was an eye-opening experience. I had known him for years as a neighbor who shared pastries, but I had never known about his heroic past. The interview humanized him in my eyes, and I gained valuable skills in patience, active listening, and navigating difficult conversations.

This experience transformed my nervousness from a personal hindrance into a potential disservice to interviewees. Rushing through interviews due to nerves could prevent them from fully sharing their stories. Preparation and the structured questions we developed helped me navigate sensitive topics and provide a platform for these veterans to share their experiences.

When we discuss media literacy and educating young people, it is crucial to allow them to see journalism from a journalist's perspective. Journalism is unique in that it doesn't always require formal certification or a degree, although I recommend one. However, a learning criteria and responsibility are essential to understand the impact of media and journalism.

Young people already possess the tools they need, such as smartphones and social media accounts, to engage with journalism. What they require is guidance on using these tools for constructive purposes, connecting with their communities, and engaging with influential figures. Encouraging them to activate their desire to be part of the journalistic community can enhance media literacy beyond discerning fact from fiction.

Media literacy encompasses more than just distinguishing real news from fake news; it involves actively participating in the news creation process. Understanding what constitutes news and being a part of its creation can eliminate doubts about its authenticity. Media literacy is woven into the fabric of our democracy, making it accessible and vital for everyone. Let us nurture and cultivate it by encouraging active participation.

Media literacy, in its true essence, transcends the mere ability to distinguish between genuine news and false information. While this skill is undoubtedly crucial, media literacy goes further by encouraging individuals to actively engage in the news creation process. It empowers people to understand not just what news is but also how it is produced, disseminated, and consumed. This comprehensive approach not only eliminates doubts about the authenticity of news but also fosters a deeper connection with the democratic ideals upon which our society is built.

At its core, media literacy is a multifaceted concept that equips individuals with the tools to critically assess, analyze, and engage with media content. It encourages them to question, probe, and verify the information presented to them, fostering a healthy skepticism that is fundamental in a world overflowing with information.

One of the key facets of media literacy is understanding what constitutes news. In a rapidly changing media landscape, where content can be generated and shared by anyone with a digital device, it's essential to grasp the principles that underlie news reporting. Media literacy teaches us to recognize the hallmarks of credible journalism, such as objectivity, verification of sources, and adherence to ethical standards.

However, media literacy doesn't stop at being a discerning consumer; it invites active participation. In an era where the line between creators and consumers of news is becoming increasingly blurred, individuals have the opportunity to contribute to the discourse. Social media platforms, citizen journalism, and user-generated content have given ordinary people a voice in shaping the news agenda.

This active engagement with news creation is not just about sharing personal opinions; it can also involve fact-checking, investigative reporting, and holding those in power accountable. It democratizes information dissemination, allowing diverse perspectives to emerge and challenging the monopoly of traditional news outlets.

Media literacy, therefore, becomes an integral part of our democratic society. It empowers citizens to be informed participants rather than passive observers. Informed citizens are better equipped to make decisions that affect their lives, communities, and the nation as a whole. They are more likely to engage in meaningful debates, contribute to positive social change, and hold public figures accountable for their actions.

In this sense, media literacy is a cornerstone of an inclusive democracy. It ensures that the benefits of critical thinking and active engagement with news are accessible to everyone, regardless of their background or level of education. It promotes transparency, trust, and civic responsibility, creating a more informed and engaged citizenry.

As we navigate an increasingly complex and interconnected media landscape, let us recognize the importance of nurturing and cultivating media literacy. It's not a skill reserved for a select few but a collective endeavor that should be encouraged and championed by educators, policymakers, and society as a whole. By promoting active participation in the news creation process, we strengthen the foundations of our democracy and ensure a brighter, more informed future for all.

Chapter Seven: Solution Oriented Reporting: Empowering Readers to Act

"Every single one of have something in us that can empower a neighbor, share it."

With the knowledge and insights gained from the book up to chapter 7, I have developed a process to initiate and facilitate change in the field of journalism. My process is designed to create a more sustainable future for journalism, both for future generations and current generations. It is my hope that this process will ensure not only the survival of the field, but also it's evolution into something even better.

I created the IPAR method to provide young writers with a structured approach to encourage narrative-based facts and community engagement. This method helps bridge the gap between data and individuals, making information more transparent and comprehensible. My goal is to reduce the amount of misinformation present today by initiating conversations around an issue and incorporating data in a relatable way. IPAR stands for Issue, Policy, Analysis, and Resources. The Issue highlights the impact of current data on affected demographics, while the Policy focuses on existing laws and conversations around them. Analysis digs deeper into the data by collaborating with experts and simplifying complex data into accessible forms. Lastly, Resources provides quotes and contributions from non-profit organizations dedicated to the issue at hand, which helps raise awareness and instigate change. By utilizing the IPAR method, stories can be crafted to engage a diverse audience, shifting the focus from sensationalism to addressing issues that affect daily lives.

A lot of what I have included in this method I created is not necessarily new, but it is designed and structured to encourage a narrative based on facts and derived from community engagement. This way, we can begin to engage our community civically and present them with information in a comprehensible manner, breaking things down so that individuals have transparency in data and understand those who generate the data. We must always incorporate these aspects into our stories as they bridge the gaps.

For instance, whenever I mention data on various platforms and in conversations, I consistently face pushback. I believe that by initiating discussions around the issues and incorporating data, making it relatable and ensuring the narratives are grounded in the "why" and "who," we can start to reduce the misinformation prevalent today. This has been a part of my goal, to establish a method for young writers.

Now, I don't believe we can evade artificial intelligence. It's still new to many, but I do think that by utilizing the IPAR method, which I'm about to explain, we can utilize prompts to better engage and bridge gaps, resulting in information that's not just created but tailored. With the vast amount of information available, there is a risk of redundancy. However, through the IPAR method, our information will possess focus, purpose, and a reason rooted in engaging our community.

Having said that, I developed the IPAR method for this purpose. The "I" stands for the issue. In my writing, I delve into the issue at hand, outlining its impact on communities according to current data. Whether it pertains to public health, community matters, legal aspects, economic development, violence, race, or any other topic, I meticulously detail the adverse effects on the most affected demographics. This demonstrates why the issue matters in historical context or based on ongoing trends.

Moving on to the "P," which represents policy. I identify any existing policies, whether in draft form or enacted as law. I also explore the ongoing conversations surrounding these policies, their status, and the legislators involved in shaping them. Whether the policies are under review, amendments are being made, or new aspects are being introduced, I ensure to highlight these changes, even extending to community rules or guidelines.

Next comes the "A" for analysis, a crucial part of the IPAR method. This involves a thorough examination of data, complete with charts and clear interpretations. Importantly, I engage with experts, reaching out to those who gathered the data or conducted research. This collaborative approach helps writers, journalists, and community members gain a deeper understanding. I believe this expertise should be leveraged to simplify complex data into accessible forms, such as charts or graphs.

Lastly, we have the "R," which stands for resources. This facet holds significant value to me. Based on past research, especially concerning topics like violence prevention, it's evident that including resources in conversations is pivotal. Non-profit organizations dedicated to specific areas play a vital role here. They possess a wealth of information and solutions related to the issues at hand. These organizations are well-connected and solution-oriented, making them ideal sources for quotes and contributions to articles. Their presence indicates that research led to their formation, which in turn enhances resources and opportunities within the community. Whether the issue revolves around health, violence, or other concerns, local and national non-profit organizations contribute to raising awareness and instigating change.

In crafting stories using this method, it doesn't cater to a single group but rather engages a diverse audience. By involving politicians, discussing policies, and highlighting data, we aim to impact everyone. This approach shifts the focus from sensationalism to addressing issues that genuinely affect our daily lives. Through the IPAR method, our central focus remains the community—always the community.

I will not bore you with a basic technically written how to on how this method is used, lets explore though the eyes of my younger self along with some current policies and data.

Here's an IPAR method article I wrote for a white paper on the impact of Illicit Fentanyl.

America has a Long-Standing Drug Problem - ISSUE

Growing up in Englewood in Chicago wasn't exactly like New Jack City, the movie. It was close though. There was the drug house, the nodding crackhead, the couple that fought and got high together, the flashy, nice car-driving drug dealers, and of course, the occasional drive-by shootings.

I remember walking south on Parnell, the blacktop paved street we used as a skating rink. But on this day, I wasn't skating. I was visiting and wanted to see my older cousin, who was at her then-boyfriend's house. So I began walking to go get her. I was alone and would take that risk at times, knowing my mother would not approve. But as I got about 10 ft from the main cross street, 69th, I heard gunshots. As I stopped and looked in total shock, a man jumped out of the car. He was shot and, holding his bleeding neck, he began shooting back at the car that had begun to speed off. Calmly, I turned around and walked back to my family's home.

Sitting on the porch, I watched chaos because the one shot was a well-known drug dealer - everyone wanted to know how badly he was hurt, and so on. I sat there watching, which is what I would often do as a kid. Like most kids, I just wanted to be a kid, but the world around me was focused on things that had nothing to do with kid stuff.

The block I grew up on that my mom moved me and my brother away from became more drug-infested, divided by poverty and drug use; the families began to separate, and we heard more stories about deaths, beatings, and jail time. By the early nineties, the War on Drugs was in full effect.

Cocaine, like opioids, started out affecting the white communities first because of access, then trickled down to the streets. The formula has not changed, only the drug.

Now there's a war on fentanyl, but it's a different type of war because its impact is widespread across many communities.

Many would argue that the war on drugs fights street drug chaos, but it doesn't stop it. Also, that addiction is winning regardless, but this war has caused over 45 million arrests due to drugs. The underlying issue for the dealers and the users is that it's all about surviving. Many experts believe that with the war on drugs and new drugs being added to the illicit market, we should not be asking why the addiction, but why the pain.

At the start of my article, I used an anecdotal lede to paint a picture of what it is like to be a part of a certain community from the perspective of a child. However, beneath the surface, the issue is much more complicated than what it appears to be. I then went on to explain how people from these communities are perceiving the problem, and outlined the various policies that are being put in place to address it. This served as an introduction to the reader, so that they can better understand the context of the issue.

Next is where I introduce what some research has gathered and the policies being formed around it.

Harm Reductive, A Different Look at Addiction - POLICY

Society is starting to shift its perspective on drug addiction and drug-related issues. Instead of perceiving addiction solely as a criminal issue, there is a growing recognition that it is a complex health issue that requires a holistic approach. Many countries have started adopting harm reduction strategies, focusing on reducing the negative consequences associated with drug use and supporting individuals in managing their substance use in a safer manner.

Harm reduction initiatives include needle exchange programs, which aim to prevent the transmission of blood-borne diseases such as HIV and hepatitis among people who inject drugs. These programs provide clean needles and syringes, along with other harm reduction supplies, as well as access to HIV testing and counseling services. By providing a safe and sterile environment for drug use, needle exchange programs not only protect the health of individuals but also contribute to the overall well-being of the community by reducing the spread of diseases.

Another harm reduction approach is the availability of naloxone, a medication that can reverse opioid overdoses and save lives. Naloxone distribution programs aim to ensure that this life-saving drug is readily accessible to individuals at risk of overdose, as well as their friends and family members. Empowering and educating the community about naloxone can significantly reduce the number of overdose deaths and provide an opportunity for individuals struggling with addiction to seek help and recovery.

Besides harm reduction, there is a growing emphasis on treatment and rehabilitation as essential components of addressing drug addiction. Instead of stigmatizing individuals with addiction, society is recognizing the importance of offering support, counseling, and access to evidence-based treatments. This includes medication-assisted treatment (MAT), which utilizes medications such as methadone or buprenorphine along with counseling and behavioral therapies to help individuals manage their opioid dependence and work towards recovery.

Additionally, there is a movement towards providing comprehensive social support systems that address the underlying factors contributing to drug addiction. Poverty, unemployment, trauma, and lack of access to education and healthcare are all factors that can contribute to substance abuse. By addressing these social determinants of drug addiction, we can create environments that foster resilience, promote mental health, and offer individuals pathways to a healthier and more fulfilling life.

The shift towards a more compassionate and comprehensive approach to drug addiction is a step in the right direction. It acknowledges the complexity of the issue and recognizes that punitive measures alone are not effective in addressing the underlying causes of addiction. By focusing on harm reduction, treatment, and social support, we can create a society that prioritizes the well-being of all its members and offers hope and healing to individuals caught in the cycle of addiction.

Illinois New Policy focusing on Harm Reduction
Illinois General Assembly: House Bill HB4334 - OVERDOSE PREVENTION FENTANYL - 1/10/2023

I introduced the bill sponsors and shared the synopsis of the Overdose Prevention and Harm Reduction Act, which had been amended. It specified that any entity providing medical care or health services may distribute fentanyl test strips to the public. My goal in sharing this was not to stir up controversy, but to demonstrate that there are different ways to engage in discussions about our communities, and that this dialogue does not have to be rooted in animosity. Doing so can help us delve into the reasons behind the various issues.

Then, I got into the data, hopefully in a way that can be digested easily, but digs into the reality of the circumstances.

Illicitly Manufactured Fentanyl Impact - ANALYSIS

The latest report from the CDC is recognizing that 110,236 people died in a single 12-month period, because of its preliminary data, we did not use it for our analysis.

We used data from the SUDORS Dashboard, in looking at data captured from 2021 by the Centers for Disease Control and Prevention. State Unintentional Drug Overdose Reporting System (SUDORS). Atlanta, GA: US Department of Health and Human Services, CDC; [2023, February 6]. Access at: https://www.cdc.gov/drugoverdose/fatal/ dashboard, we sift out facts among the death information available in medical examiner and coroner reports.

The data presented in the 2021 SUDORS dashboard sheds light on the devastating impact of illicitly manufactured fentanyl (IMFs) and the opioid crisis in the United States. With a total of 50,943 reported overdose deaths from 32 jurisdictions, this dataset provides valuable insights into the magnitude of the problem.

Among the states heavily affected by IMFs, West Virginia and Washington DC stand out, with rates of 69.0 and 63.2 deaths per 100,000 population, respectively. IMFs accounted for the majority of opioids involved in these tragic deaths, representing a staggering 72.7% of all reported cases, amounting to 37,017 deaths.

Analyzing the temporal patterns of overdose deaths, it is evident that the months of March, April, and May experienced the highest number of fatalities. However, there was a slight dip in June only to see the numbers rise again in July. These fluctuations underscore the urgent need for comprehensive interventions and effective strategies throughout the year to address this crisis.

When examining the demographic characteristics of those affected by overdose deaths, it is important to note that gender and age play significant roles. Men account for a higher percentage (29.7%) of deaths due to IMFs compared to women (70.3%). The age group most impacted by these fatalities is 35-44 (26.0%), closely followed by those aged 25-34 (23.1%). While men are primarily affected in the 25-34 age group (23.6%), both men and women face equal risks in the 35-44 age category (26.0%).

Regarding race and ethnicity, the data reveals that 67.9% of overdose deaths were among individuals identified as White, non-Hispanic, while 19.2% were among those identified as Black, non-Hispanic. However, when we consider the rate of overdose deaths per 100,000 persons within each racial/ethnic group, the disparity becomes more pronounced. The rate among Black, non-Hispanic individuals rises to 50.8%, whereas it decreases to 35.0% for White, non-Hispanic individuals.

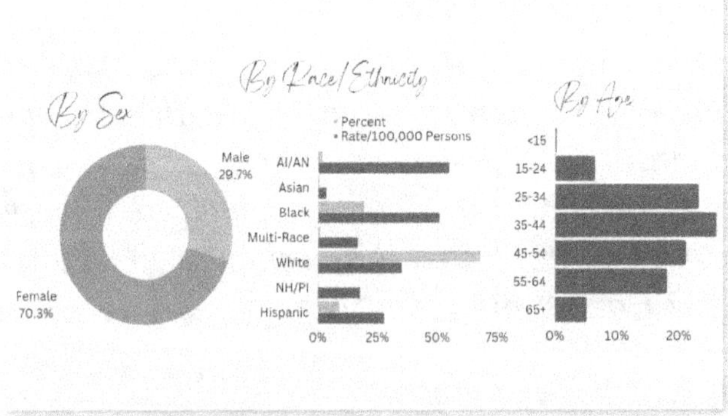

These statistics highlight the alarming impact of the opioid crisis, particularly in relation to IMFs, and emphasize the urgent need for coordinated efforts to address this public health emergency. By raising awareness, improving access to treatment and harm reduction services, and implementing comprehensive prevention strategies, communities can work towards combating the opioid epidemic and ultimately saving lives.

Circumstances matter most when it comes to prevention and what this particular data show is that 46.1% of these death occurrences had a bystander present and 20.2% had naloxone administered. These figures emphasize the critical importance of timely interventions and the potential impact they can have on saving lives.

At this point in the article, I decided to include additional information and resources related to the bill I discussed previously. I provided the reader with some terms and definitions, however, I left out organizations that offer naloxone and harm reduction training. I opted not to include them in this instance, but to provide a complete example, here is the resource component related to the article.

We All Can Play a Part in Fixing This - RESOURCES

Having a bystander present during an overdose can be a crucial factor in preventing fatalities. Their presence allows for immediate action, such as calling emergency services or administering life-saving measures like naloxone. Naloxone, also known as Narcan, is a medication used to rapidly reverse the effects of opioid overdose. By administering naloxone, the chances of survival increase significantly, giving the individual a fighting chance to overcome the overdose.

These statistics shed light on the positive impact that awareness and preparedness can have in the face of such a crisis. It is vital for individuals, communities, and healthcare providers to stay informed about the signs of overdose and to have naloxone readily available. Education campaigns and training initiatives can play a key role in empowering people to take immediate action when confronted with an overdose situation.

Because of the new law, harm reduction can be carried out more efficiently in Illinois. This is also why the war on fentanyl looks different than the war on drugs from the eighties far into the 2000s because the approach seems to be about saving the life of the users, which is a divergent approach.

Naloxone is less controversial; it is a medication approved by the Food and Drug Administration (FDA) designed to rapidly reverse opioid overdose. It is an opioid antagonist—meaning that it binds to opioid receptors and can reverse and block the effects of other opioids, such as heroin, morphine, and oxycodone. Administered when a patient is showing signs of opioid overdose, naloxone is a temporary treatment, and its effects do not last long.

Fentanyl test strips (FTS) are what the new legislation is shaped around. It is a low-cost method of helping prevent drug overdoses and reducing harm. FTS are small strips of paper that can detect the presence of fentanyl in all different kinds of drugs (cocaine, methamphetamine, heroin, etc.) and drug forms (pills, powder, and injectables).

The more we know, the better we can serve our community. Also, the more likely we are to show *compassion. Substance use awareness also helps debunk stigmas.*

The IPAR method has proven to be an effective framework for initiating and facilitating positive change in the field of journalism. By creating a structured approach that encourages narrative-based facts and community engagement, this method addresses the challenges faced by modern journalism. The process not only ensures the survival of the field but also paves the way for its evolution into something more impactful and meaningful.

The IPAR method, with its four key components—Issue, Policy, Analysis, and Resources—serves as a comprehensive guide to crafting stories that resonate with diverse audiences. By delving into the heart of issues, considering existing policies and conversations, analyzing complex data with expert insights, and incorporating resources from non-profit organizations, this method bridges the gap between information and individuals. It allows for transparent, comprehensible information that promotes civic engagement and informed decision-making.

Through the lens of the IPAR method, I execute an article on the impact of illicit fentanyl, showcasing how this framework can be applied in practice. By combining personal narratives, policy insights, data analysis, and resource information, the article provides a well-rounded perspective on a critical issue. In this, I demonstrate the power of initiating conversations and awunderstanding the "why" and "who" behind data, which is essential in combating misinformation and fostering informed discourse.

This method not only addresses the immediate issue at hand but also contributes to the broader shift in journalism toward a more compassionate and comprehensive approach. By prioritizing community engagement, focusing on solutions, and fostering understanding, the IPAR method ensures that journalism remains relevant and valuable in today's dynamic information landscape. As I continue to refine and apply this method, it's my hope that it reshape the narrative surrounding various issues and create a more informed, empathetic society.

I completely understand the frustration and concern that arises from the abundance of unreliable information in today's media landscape. It's disheartening to see the negative impacts it has on trust and engagement. Having access to trustworthy sources is crucial for individuals to feel confident in the information they consume. When we can rely on accurate and reliable information, it allows for more meaningful engagement and a deeper understanding of the world around us. Overcoming the challenges of sensationalism is essential to rebuilding trust and fostering a more informed society.

Knowledge is a powerful tool that has the ability to empower individuals and create positive change in our society. It is through the acquisition of knowledge that people can become agents of change, shaping a world that embraces diversity and inclusion. By fostering a shared sense of empowerment, we can build a society that uplifts and includes everyone.

When we see ourselves, our experiences, and our reality portrayed deeply, honestly, and clearly in the media, it inspires us to become more involved. This sense of inclusion is incredibly powerful.

The portrayal of ourselves, our experiences, and our reality in the media is not merely a reflection but a profound influence on our perception of the world and our role within it. When the media authentically and transparently represents the diversity of human experiences and perspectives, it has the remarkable power to inspire us to become more deeply engaged in society. This sense of inclusion is not just powerful; it is transformative.

Authentic representation in the media holds a mirror up to our lives and shows us that our stories matter. It reaffirms our identities and validates our experiences. It tells us that we are seen and heard, that our struggles and triumphs are acknowledged and celebrated. This recognition fosters a profound sense of belonging and pride, reinforcing our connection to the broader community and society at large.

When we witness ourselves portrayed honestly in the media, it goes beyond superficial recognition. It provides a platform for empathy and understanding. It bridges gaps of ignorance and misconceptions, allowing people from different backgrounds to relate to one another on a fundamental human level. It fosters compassion and solidarity, as we recognize our shared humanity in the stories of others.

Honest media representation serves as a source of inspiration. It shows us that we can aspire to achieve great things, overcome adversity, and make a meaningful impact. When we see individuals who look like us, come from similar backgrounds, or face similar challenges achieving success or advocating for positive change, it ignites a spark within us. It fuels our aspirations and motivates us to pursue our goals, knowing that we are not alone in our endeavors.

This sense of inclusion in the media also extends to our communities. When our neighborhoods, cultures, and traditions are showcased with respect and authenticity, it instills a sense of pride and ownership. It encourages us to actively engage in preserving and enriching our cultural heritage. We become more invested in the well-being of our communities, fostering a collective sense of responsibility and empowerment.

In essence, the power of inclusive media representation lies in its ability to spark hope and galvanize people into action. It takes our individual stories and celebrates our unique identities, creating a platform for connection and solidarity. It reminds us that we have the power to shape our own destinies, to create positive and lasting change, and to stand in solidarity to demand justice. It is an essential tool for inspiring people to embrace and share their truth, to find courage in their shared experiences, and to stand up for the rights of all people, regardless of race, gender, sexual orientation, or economic status. Through inclusive media representation, individuals and communities are empowered to create a better, more equitable world.

As we consume media, we have to acknowledge that we can play an active role in supporting and advocating for diverse and honest representation. By demanding authenticity, celebrating inclusive storytelling, and amplifying underrepresented voices, we contribute to a more equitable and empowering media landscape—one that continues to inspire and unite us all.

Chapter Eight: The Future of Journalism: Compassion Realized

Entering the realm of possibility can be a daunting prospect. The idea that we could inhabit a world marked by compassion can sometimes seem distant, even draining. In our current society, the prevalence of negativity both online and offline can cast a shadow over our hopes. Yet, within this complex landscape, there exists an extraordinary potential for individuals to extend compassion towards one another.

Imagine a world where compassion is commonplace, where the simplest gestures are illuminated by kindness. Picture driving down a road and experiencing a shift in perspective when someone cuts you off or speeds past you. Rather than irritation, you begin to consider the possibility that their urgency might stem from an unseen disadvantage —an elder needing to run errands during their limited travel window, perhaps between 9:00 AM and 3:00 PM. Instead of frustration, you cultivate patience, recognizing their needs. These are the seemingly inconsequential moments we often overlook in our haste—a rush to work, the drudgery of household chores, the daily routine.

It's from these unassuming interactions that the foundation of compassion can grow. Perhaps it's lending a helping hand, offering a genuine smile, or assisting with a seemingly minor task. It's in these simple deeds that we lay the groundwork for a more inclusive community, one that thrives on empathy and mutual support.

Of course, there's a twinge of fear that accompanies the aspiration to forge such a community. The fear that we may never truly arrive at our envisioned destination can loom large. Yet, this trepidation is not unwelcome—it's a sign of our desire for progress. But remember, this fear is not insurmountable. It can be overcome by focusing on the small victories, the everyday acts of compassion that may seem insignificant on their own but, over time, accumulate into a collective force of change.

The journey towards a compassionate society is not one of grand gestures but of small, deliberate actions. It's about seizing opportunities that might otherwise slip through our fingers—the smiles unshared, the hands not extended, the kind words left unsaid. By infusing these moments with intention, we can foster a spirit of compassion that ripples through our interactions and shapes our communities.

So, let us embrace the fear with open arms, knowing that it's a catalyst for growth. Let's nurture the potential for a more compassionate world by tending to the small, overlooked corners of our lives. Each smile, each act of kindness, each moment of patience contributes to a collective transformation—one that brings us closer to the inclusive, compassionate community we yearn for.

Redefining Perspective: Embracing Authenticity and Compassion

It's not just about superficial awareness; it's about delving into the intricacies of the seemingly minor aspects. We need to fully comprehend the importance of paying attention to these subtleties. Yet, it's not solely about noticing them; it's also about unraveling the profound "why" that underlies our actions. From the very beginning, I emphasized the significance of understanding the "why" – the driving force behind our decisions, actions, and even our failures to connect with one another. Often, we tend to overlook or dismiss the "why" as something trivial, but in reality, it holds profound depth.

Consider the word "why." It may be short in letters, but its significance goes beyond its brevity. Understanding our own "why" can be challenging, let alone attempting to grasp the motivations of others. Yet, it's an essential journey, one that leads us to a place of wisdom and empathy. Imagine looking at the world through the diverse lenses of others – a perspective shaped by their experiences, circumstances, and identities. This is where we exist, where we live our lives. To genuinely comprehend others, we must first understand ourselves.

To truly see the world outside, we must start from the inside – with a clear self-awareness that doesn't ignore our own struggles and challenges. By addressing our own issues, we can open our eyes to the external matters we often overlook. It's a transformation that enables us to shift from being self-focused to embracing our neighbors and community. It's not that we lack care for them; it's simply that we sometimes forget the "why" behind their actions and experiences.

Acknowledging the "why" requires us to confront the complexities of our own lives. It's tempting to evade difficulties, to sweep problems under the rug, and pretend they don't exist. But that's not authenticity; it's self-deception. The path to authenticity involves looking at our personal challenges and embracing them head-on. It's through this internal journey that we find the strength to engage with the world around us.

Consider this: I wrote an entire book advocating for compassion and inclusion. However, these ideals remain unrealistic if we aren't authentic with ourselves. Authenticity is the cornerstone; it's how we discover our purpose, set goals, and become the genuine individuals motivational speakers encourage us to be. The practice of journalism can certainly carry the weight of reshaping our society, but it cannot do so alone. It requires us to individually embark on a task of self-discovery – an internal "feng shui," if you will.

Let this workbook guide you as you uncover your own "why," fostering authenticity and compassion. By acknowledging your own journey, you lay the groundwork for understanding the world through diverse perspectives. Remember, change starts from within. As we each embrace our authenticity, we pave the way for a more compassionate world, where journalism becomes a vessel for transformation and understanding.

Journaling Ideas:
1. Reflect on a time when understanding the "why" behind your actions led to a deeper understanding of yourself or others.
2. How does practicing authenticity influence your ability to connect with others and engage in compassionate actions?

3. Share an experience where addressing your own challenges allowed you to see external issues with greater clarity.

4. Consider your personal journey towards authenticity. How has it impacted your perception of the world and your relationships?

5. What steps can you take to foster a more compassionate world by aligning your actions with your authentic self?

The Future of Journalism

I recently delved into envisioning a more compassionate future for society, pondering what that might entail. It all starts with us, within ourselves. Our journey begins by embracing the idea of self-improvement, shifting our perspective away from selfishness and towards empathy, viewing the world through the eyes of others. It's about acknowledging the suffering and challenges that exist and extending a helping hand.

All of these ideas are genuinely inspiring, and I earnestly wish to witness their realization in my lifetime. However, there's another aspiration that burns within me—an earnest desire to witness a resurgence of respect for the field of journalism. I yearn to see journalism regarded as an institution that nurtures and amplifies the wealth of great ideas within our society.

My perspective is grounded in my experiences within urban, suburban, and even somewhat rural settings. While I understand that there are diverse community makeups beyond my own encounters, I firmly believe that every community, in its unique way, possesses a vision that journalism can help bring to fruition. After all, writing, storytelling, and creation are universal endeavors, necessitating the sharing of different stories, perspectives, viewpoints, and belief systems.

In a world that was designed to be the "land of the free" but has often fallen short, we continually strive to refine the experiment in each generation. Yet, I firmly believe that achieving this vision is impossible without upholding the integrity of journalism. It's a vital instrument that must begin with our young people and children, imparting the core principles and values of journalism so they, too, can respect and carry it forward into the future.

In recent times, with the advent of technologies like artificial intelligence, there has been concern that journalism's importance may diminish. As technology generates words at an astonishing rate, it can make individuals question the relevance of human contributions. This dilemma is one educators and professionals in various fields grapple with. Personally, when I started my career in journalism, I contemplated abandoning it due to the rise of social media and the emergence of bloggers and vloggers who seemed to render traditional journalism obsolete. After all, everyone had a smartphone, eliminating the need for photographers and reporters.

The first industry I believed technology would disrupt was journalism. However, here I am, well over a decade into my career path, advocating for the revitalization and preservation of journalism's core value in our society. The art of journalism cannot be erased; it's an integral part of our culture. Instead, we must work to improve and adapt it to our changing world.

I firmly believe that we must invest in and support local media because that's where journalism truly matters. While big media organizations may garner the bulk of ad revenue and viewership, we should not be intimidated by their financial might or new technologies. If we succumb to such fears, journalism could disappear before our eyes, becoming a relic of the past. Instead, we should strive to sustain it, especially at the local level, where it can make the most significant impact.

While I don't often delve into politics, especially when covering the presidency, I am confident that the press will remain an integral part of our democracy. However, it's crucial to recognize our role in shaping the community on a local level. It's time we emphasize the importance of local journalism, cultivating news that empowers people to make informed decisions and participate in meaningful ways.

I am optimistic that journalism can be a force that revitalizes and strengthens our communities, particularly at the grassroots level. It's time to elevate the value of journalism and its critical role in our society.

Delving into the role of media, we often have to remind ourselves of the First Amendment. We often hear about it but seldom reflect on its words: "Congress shall make no law respecting an establishment of religion, or prohibiting the free exercise thereof; or abridging the freedom of speech, or of the press; or the right of the people peaceably to assemble, and to petition the government for a redress of grievances."

These protections specifically apply to criticizing and scrutinizing the government or those with significant responsibility over governmental affairs. It's essential to differentiate what's protected and what's not. We must discern between reliable sources and those spreading falsehoods.

Now, let's explore the role of media, which encompasses various functions. Information serves to satisfy curiosity and reduce uncertainty about the world. However, in our age of information overload, accuracy can sometimes be compromised due to the rush to be the first to report.

Interpretation involves presenting current events with subjective commentary based on personal feelings and opinions. Instructive media educates, cultivating knowledge through various channels like documentaries and educational TV. Bonding media brings like-minded people together, fostering communities with shared values and interests.

Additionally, media offers diversion, a crucial function that allows us to escape our daily lives temporarily. It's essential to strike a balance between being informed and taking breaks for entertainment and relaxation.

Media also acts as a gatekeeper, providing a filter for information. Streaming services and reputable platforms play this role, offering curated content that is more reliable and vetted.

We already discussed media literacy and that Illinois passed a bill mandating media literacy education in public high schools, beginning in the 2022-2023 school year. Media literacy involves the ability to assess, analyze, evaluate, create, and communicate through various forms of media, which we already talked about in detail.

Its good to bring it up again to reiterate that the curriculum should cover assessing information, analyzing and evaluating media messages, creating media, reflecting on media consumption, understanding social responsibility and civics, and engaging in respectful, fact-based dialogues on specific issues.

We talked about the other areas that came about through social media, but it's essential that professionals in the media field play a role in crafting this curriculum, as their expertise can help ensure unbiased instruction.

Will, I help in that, I sure hope so.

As we discussed the evolving landscape of media and the vital role that media literacy plays in education, it becomes evident that professionals in the media field should be actively engaged in shaping this curriculum. Their expertise is invaluable, not only in crafting the curriculum but also in ensuring that it delivers unbiased and comprehensive instruction.

Media professionals possess firsthand knowledge of the media industry's inner workings, its nuances, and the challenges it faces. They are intimately familiar with the ethical dilemmas, the potential for bias, and the ever-evolving nature of media content and technology. As such, their insights are crucial in developing a curriculum that equips students with the tools to critically assess and navigate the media landscape.

One primary reason for involving media professionals in curriculum development is their ability to provide real-world context. They can share concrete examples of media manipulation, the consequences of misinformation, and the ethical dilemmas journalists and media organizations grapple with regularly. These real-life stories and experiences can make the curriculum more relatable and engaging for students, helping them understand the practical applications of media literacy.

Moreover, media professionals can contribute to the curriculum by addressing emerging media trends and technologies. With the media landscape constantly evolving, staying up-to-date is challenging but essential. Media experts can help educators incorporate relevant and timely topics, such as the impact of social media algorithms, deepfake technology, and the role of artificial intelligence in content creation, into the curriculum. By doing so, students can better prepare themselves for the media challenges of the future.

Another critical aspect of media professionals' involvement is their ability to foster critical thinking. They can guide students in analyzing media content from various sources, identifying potential biases, fact-checking information, and discerning between credible and unreliable sources. These skills are not only essential for media literacy but also for active and informed citizenship.

Media professionals can emphasize the importance of responsible media consumption and ethical reporting. They can provide valuable insights into the ethical dilemmas faced by journalists and content creators, discussing issues like sensationalism, privacy concerns, and the responsibility to report the truth. By instilling ethical principles early on, students can develop a strong foundation for responsible media engagement.

The involvement of media professionals in shaping media literacy curriculum is not just beneficial; it is essential. Their expertise ensures that the curriculum remains relevant, unbiased, and responsive to the dynamic nature of the media landscape. With their guidance, students can develop the critical thinking skills and ethical awareness needed to navigate today's media-saturated world effectively.

About the Author

I have to admit that in the post-COVID-pandemic era, I am a completely different person. That time required me to slow down and evaluate my purpose, mission, and what I'd like to accomplish. I had to take a good look at the pace at which I was working to achieve my goals and it was unreal. I feel that we all had an opportunity to truly evaluate if our actions serve a greater good, and from that, we have to recalibrate. So, in this moment, I am living in the recalibration, hoping that I will manifest my goals in a more fulfilling and rewarding way.